Weird Wessex

A Tourist Guide to 100 Strange and Unusual Sights

Paul Jackson
&
Andrew May

WEIRD WESSEX

Published in Great Britain by CFZ Press 2015

Copyright © 2015 by Centre for Fortean Zoology

Text copyright © by Paul Jackson & Andrew May

All images copyright © Paul Jackson & Andrew May unless otherwise stated

The right of Paul Jackson and Andrew May to be identified as the authors of this work has been asserted by them in accordance with the Copyright, Designs and Patents Act 1988.

All rights reserved. Without limiting the rights under copyright reserved above, no part of this publication may be reproduced, stored in or introduced into a retrieval system, or transmitted, in any form or by any means (electronic, mechanical, photocopying, recording or otherwise), without the prior written permission of the publisher and authors, nor be otherwise circulated in any form of binding or cover other than that in which it is published and without a similar condition being imposed on the subsequent purchaser.

ISBN: 978-1-909488-35-9

CFZ Press
Myrtle Cottage
Woolsery
Bideford
North Devon
EX39 5QR

www.cfzpublishing.co.uk

Contents

Contents 3

Introduction 7

1   Weird Archaeology... 9

    1.1   *Cheddar Gorge* 10

    1.2   *Stonehenge* 12

    1.3   *The Avebury Complex* 14

    1.4   *Stanton Drew Stone Circle* 17

    1.5   *Uffington* 19

    1.6   *The Hell Stone* 21

    1.7   *Roman Bath* 22

    1.8   *Dorchester*... 24

    1.9   *Glastonbury Abbey*.. 26

    1.10   *Kingston Lacy* 28

2   Weird Buildings 29

    2.1   *Wells Cathedral*... 30

    2.2   *Stockwood Church* 32

    2.3   *Wilton Church* 33

    2.4   *Wickham Church*... 35

    2.5   *St Aldhelm's Chapel* 37

    2.6   *The Hanging Chapel* 38

    2.7   *Castle Drogo*.. 39

    2.8   *Lyme Regis Museum* 40

    2.9   *Chesapeake Mill* 42

    2.10   *The House that Moved* 44

3 Weird Constructions 45

- 3.1 Maud Heath's Causeway 46
- 3.2 The Combe Gibbet 48
- 3.3 The Temples of Stourhead 49
- 3.4 Horton Tower 52
- 3.5 Farley Mount 54
- 3.6 Portsmouth Sea Forts 55
- 3.7 The Portuguese Fireplace 57
- 3.8 Kilve Oil Retort 58
- 3.9 Kimmeridge Oil Well 59
- 3.10 Solstice Park 60

4 Weird History 63

- 4.1 Dead Man's Plack 64
- 4.2 The Rufus Stone 65
- 4.3 Ludgershall Castle 66
- 4.4 The Remedy Oak 68
- 4.5 Weymouth's Cannonball 69
- 4.6 The Battle of Alton 71
- 4.7 The Monmouth Rebellion 73
- 4.8 Sedgemoor Battlefield 74
- 4.9 A Relic of the Napoleonic Wars 76
- 4.10 Morwellham Quay 78

5 Weird Landscape 79

- 5.1 Old Sarum 80
- 5.2 Danebury Hill-Fort 82
- 5.3 Maiden Castle 83
- 5.4 Ham Hill 85
- 5.5 Westbury White Horse 86
- 5.6 Alton Barnes 87
- 5.7 The Cerne Giant 89

Contents

	5.8	Osmington White Horse	91
	5.9	Broad Town White Horse	93
	5.10	The Undercliff	94

6 Weird Legends ... 97

	6.1	The Brutus Stone	98
	6.2	Plymouth Hoe	100
	6.3	Glastonbury Tor	102
	6.4	Cadbury Castle	104
	6.5	Winchester's Round Table	106
	6.6	King Alfred's Monument	108
	6.7	The Devil's Stone	110
	6.8	The Tedworth Drummer	111
	6.9	Sweet Fanny Adams	112
	6.10	The Snake Catcher's Grave	114

7 Weird Religion ... 115

	7.1	Knowlton Church and Earthworks	116
	7.2	Whitchurch Canonicorum	117
	7.3	A Mediaeval Dragon-Slayer	120
	7.4	Langton Cross	121
	7.5	The Angels of Muchelney	122
	7.6	The Meditation Chair	124
	7.7	Martin's Ape	126
	7.8	The Nether Wallop Pyramid	127
	7.9	Portesham's Inside-Out Tomb	129
	7.10	The Virgin Crowns	130

8 Weird Science ... 133

	8.1	The Dorset Dinosaur	134
	8.2	The Flying Monk	135
	8.3	Mediaeval Timekeeping	138
	8.4	Frankenstein's Creator	140

8.5	Chard's Aviation Pioneer	141
8.6	Brean Down Fort	143
8.7	The Bouncing Bomb	145
8.8	A Pioneer of Psychical Research	147
8.9	The Warminster Thing	149
8.10	Crop Circle Country	151
9	**Weird Secrets**	**153**
9.1	Ghost Town	154
9.2	The Deserted Village	156
9.3	The Artificial Lake	158
9.4	Beer Quarry Caves	160
9.5	Dunster Castle	162
9.6	The GHQ Line	164
9.7	The Verne Citadel	167
9.8	The Bunker in the Woods	169
9.9	Royal Signals Museum	171
9.10	The Man who Created James Bond	172
10	**Weird Tales**	**173**
10.1	Sherborne Castles	174
10.2	An Explorer and a Poet	176
10.3	The Ancient Mariner	178
10.4	Dartmoor	180
10.5	Montacute House	182
10.6	Lawrence of Arabia	184
10.7	The Mummy's Curse	186
10.8	Mystery Island	188
10.9	The Ring of Silvianus	190
10.10	The Dalek Caves	192
Index		**195**

Introduction

At its height, the Saxon kingdom of Wessex sprawled across Southern England, encompassing Wiltshire, Hampshire, Dorset, Somerset and parts of Devon and Berkshire. Even before the Saxons arrived the area had a reputation as a weird place, with Stonehenge and its Druids, Glastonbury and the Holy Grail, the bizarre chalk figure of the Cerne Giant and the reputed location of King Arthur's Camelot. In more recent times the tradition of weirdness has continued, with flying saucers sighted over Warminster, intricate Crop Circles popping up around Alton Barnes and hordes of spaced-out hippies converging on the mystical hubs of Glastonbury and Totnes.

This book is a tourist guide with a difference. It describes 100 of the weirdest sights in Wessex, ranging from world-famous places like Glastonbury and Stonehenge to hidden oddities that may even surprise the locals. It is divided into ten thematic chapters, each describing ten sites across the region: Weird Archaeology, Weird Buildings, Weird Constructions, Weird History, Weird Landscape, Weird Legends, Weird Religion, Weird Science, Weird Secrets and Weird Tales!

1 Weird Archaeology

In broad terms, archaeology refers to the art and science of digging up relics from past cultures. The Wessex region is particularly rich in archaeological remains, many of which seem pretty weird when viewed from a present-day perspective.

The ten sites in this chapter are arranged roughly in chronological order. The Old Stone Age (Palaeolithic) and Middle Stone Age (Mesolithic) periods are represented by the caves of Cheddar Gorge, while the New Stone Age (Neolithic) and Bronze Age saw the great megalithic constructions of Stonehenge, Avebury, Stanton Drew and Uffington, as well as Dorset's more modest "Hell Stone". Reminders of Roman times can be found in Bath and Dorchester, while more recent takes on archaeology can be seen at Glastonbury and Kingston Lacy.

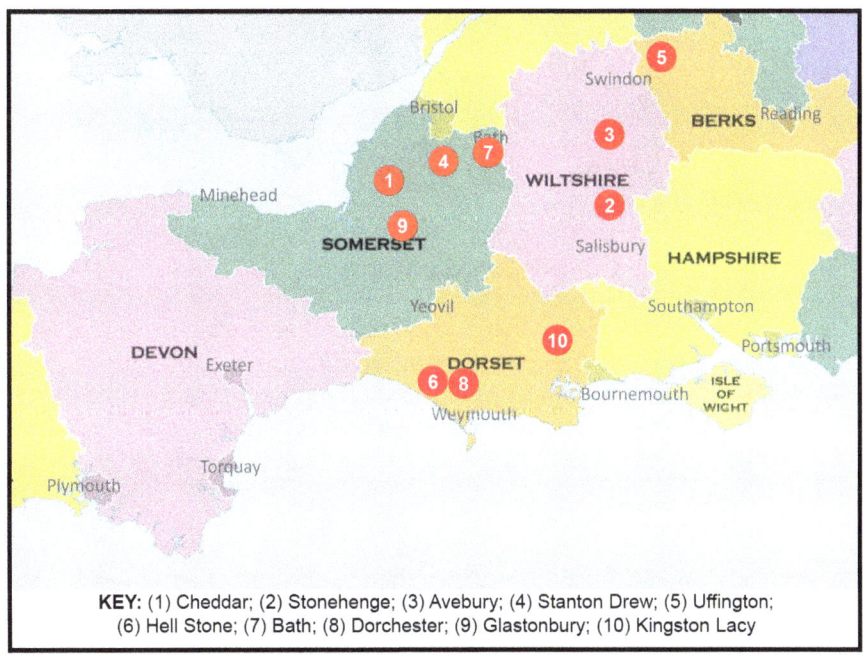

Locator map for Weird Archaeology

1.1 Cheddar Gorge

Satnav: Cheddar, Somerset BS27 3QF (admission charge to caves)

Today, the caves of Cheddar Gorge are one of the top tourist attractions in Somerset. For thousands of years, however, prehistoric people thought of them as home. In fact the earliest inhabitants of the caves weren't even modern humans, but Neanderthals – they lived in Cheddar from perhaps 40,000 BC to 24,000 BC, when the region froze over in the Ice Age. The Neanderthals were forced to move south, and they never came back.

Cheddar Gorge

The next period of occupation was a brief interglacial period around 12,700 BC. These inhabitants were modern humans – *homo sapiens* – of the Palaeolithic or Old Stone Age period. Deep inside one of the caves, known as Gough's Cave, tourists can see a wall carving of a mammoth that was produced around this time – the oldest known work of art in the British Isles.

Fragmentary human remains from the period around 12,700 BC have been found inside Gough's Cave, including skulls and other bones from a young child, two older children and two adults. All these remains showed tool-marks that strongly suggest butchery – it appears that Cheddar's inhabitants at that time were cannibals!

Weird Archaeology

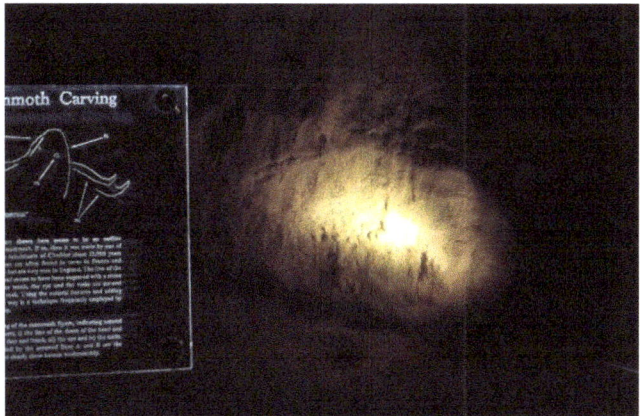
The Mammoth carving

Soon afterwards the cold weather came back, and people were forced to migrate south again. It was only when the ice sheet finally receded around 8000 BC that *homo sapiens* returned to the area. By this time human civilization had progressed to a new era – the Mesolithic, or Middle Stone Age. This was a time of hunter-gatherers, and the oldest complete skeleton ever found in Britain dates from this period. It was discovered in Gough's Cave in 1903, and is now known as "Cheddar Man".

A replica of Cheddar Man in situ in Gough's Cave

1.2 Stonehenge

Satnav: Stonehenge, Wiltshire SP4 7DE (English Heritage)

Stonehenge, in Wiltshire, is one of the most famous prehistoric sites in the world. The arrangement of the stones that can be seen today probably dates from the middle of the Bronze Age, around 1600 BC. However, this was just the culmination of a long period of expansion and development which began in Neolithic times and continued for at least 1500 years.

Stonehenge

The oldest stones at Stonehenge are the bluestones, which arrived at the site around 2600 BC from Preseli Mountain in south-west Wales, some 240 miles away. These were joined two or three hundred years later by the massive sarsen stones, each weighing over 25 tonnes, which were brought from the Marlborough Downs 20 miles to the north.

The stones were arranged in two concentric circles – an outer circle of sarsens and an inner circle of bluestones. Inside the inner circle was a horseshoe of sarsens, and finally an innermost horseshoe of bluestones. This arrangement can still be discerned today, although many of the sarsens have now toppled over, and most of the bluestones have been removed over the years to be reused for other purposes.

Stonehenge differs from Britain's numerous other stone circles in two important respects. First, all of the stones making up the circle have been squared and dressed, like a classical stone temple. Secondly, the upright stones are topped with horizontal lintel stones, held in place with mortise-and-tenon joints. This again gives an impression closer to a Greek or Roman temple than a prehistoric structure.

Early theories about the origin of Stonehenge often assumed that it was indeed a classical temple, and many antiquarians confidently asserted that it had been dedicated to Apollo or Bacchus, or even the Buddha. Its construction was attributed to great civilizations of the past such as the Phoenicians or Romans, although these were much more recent than the actual date of the building.

Perhaps the most famous theory of Stonehenge is that it was the work of the Druids – the priestly class who presided over Britain in pre-Roman times. The association between Stonehenge and the Druids was popularized by the antiquarian William Stukeley in the 18th century – and remains popular to this day, although in fact Stonehenge would have been an ancient ruin even in Druid times. Nevertheless, it is possible that Druid priests re-used the stone circle for their own rituals.

Stukeley's conception of Stonehenge in Druid times
(public domain image)

In recent years, Stonehenge has become a symbol of the neo-Pagan movement, and today it is just as likely to attract hippies and New Agers as archaeologists and antiquarians. The stones are famously aligned with the direction of the rising sun on the morning of the summer solstice, 21 June, and as a consequence Stonehenge has become the site of huge celebrations on that day each year. An estimated 37,000 people attended the event in 2014, many of them self-identifying as "Druids" or "Pagans".

1.3 The Avebury Complex

Satnav: Avebury, Wiltshire SN8 1RG (National Trust)

The area surrounding the village of Avebury in Wiltshire is known around the world for its mystical landscape, including the Avebury Henge, Silbury Hill and the West Kennet Long Barrow. These impressive relics of the Neolithic age can all be found near the A4 trunk road as it winds its way between Marlborough and Calne.

Avebury Henge itself, constructed between 2850 BC and 2200 BC, is an impressively large monument consisting of a bank and ditch system with three stone circles – an outer circle and two inner circles – enclosing a total area of 28.5 acres. The site is divided by four entrances that cut through the earthworks. Today the bank is between 4.2 and 5.4 metres high, but it was originally an estimated 17 metres high accompanied by a 9 metre deep ditch. It is believed the banks and ditch originally consisted of exposed chalk, giving the earthworks a striking white appearance.

The outer circle of stones has a diameter of approximately 332 metres, making it Britain's largest stone circle and one of the biggest in Europe. This outer circle is believed to have originally consisted of 98 to 105 sarsen stones, of different sizes and shapes – the tallest around 4.2 metres high and the heaviest over 40 tonnes.

A section of the Avebury Henge stone circle

Weird Archaeology

The centre of the Avebury site consists of two smaller separate stone circles. The northern circle measures 98 metres in diameter and is believed to have originally consisted of 27 standing stones, of which only 4 remain in situ today. The southern circle was 108 metres in diameter and is believed to have originally consisted of 27 standing stones centred on "The Great Obelisk" – a large sarsen up to 6.4 metres tall. The southern circle was destroyed in the 18th century and today the location of the Great Obelisk is marked with a concrete post.

One of the Avebury sarsen stones

Another striking feature of the Avebury landscape is Silbury Hill – an artificial mound sitting at the side of the A4 road. It was constructed around 2400 BC using half a million tonnes of chalk and clay. Standing an impressive 40 metres high, with a width of 167 metres at the base and 30 metres at the summit, Silbury Hill is the largest prehistoric man-made mound in Europe.

Silbury Hill

The construction of the mound was a significant undertaking, with estimates ranging from 4 to 18 million man-hours. The original purpose of the hill remains a mystery. Archaeological excavations made from the 17th century onwards have included a vertical shaft from the top of the hill down through to its base, and a horizontal tunnel at the base all the way to the centre. None of these excavations have been able to establish the hill's purpose with any certainty.

The oldest surviving structure in the Avebury complex is the West Kennet Long Barrow, which was constructed around 3650 BC – pre-dating Stonehenge by about 400 years. The barrow is one of the largest Neolithic tombs in Britain, at approximately 3.2 metres in height, 25 metres in width and 100 metres in length. The barrow sits atop a chalk ridge and commands a good view of Silbury Hill and other features of the local landscape. In its original form, the barrow's sides would have been bare white chalk, making it a very prominent place for people to be buried. When explored by archaeologists, it was found to contain at least forty-six burials, ranging from those of infants to the elderly.

Inside West Kennet Long Barrow

1.4 Stanton Drew Stone Circle

Satnav: Stanton Drew, Somerset BS39 4EW (English Heritage)

Perhaps the most remarkable thing about the stone circle that resides in the village of Stanton Drew in Somerset is that so few people have heard of it! At 113 metres in diameter, it is the second largest stone circle in Britain after Avebury – and considerably larger than the circle at Stonehenge. Like Avebury and Stonehenge, the Stanton Drew circle was constructed during the late Neolithic and early Bronze Age periods, between 3000 and 2000 BC.

The Great Circle at Stanton Drew

The large stone circle at Stanton Drew is known as the "Great Circle", to distinguish it from two smaller circles nearby, one to the south-west (43 metres diameter) and the other to the north-east (30 metres diameter). Taken together, the Stanton Drew complex constitutes the third largest megalithic site in England, after its much more famous rivals at Avebury and Stonehenge.

One of the reasons for Stanton Drew's relative obscurity is that, despite its size, it is far less impressive to the eye than Stonehenge or Avebury. The stones are much smaller, many of them have toppled over, and the overall circular plan is difficult to discern today.

Another view of Stanton Drew

As with Stonehenge, historians of the 18th century, such as William Stukeley, believed the Stanton Drew complex to have been the work of the ancient Druids. In this case, there is even an apparent clue in the name of the village! However, *deru* – the old spelling of Drew – was a common Celtic word meaning oak, so this may be no more than coincidence. That hasn't stopped the local pub calling itself the Druid's Arms, though!

The South-West Circle at Stanton Drew

1.5 Uffington

Satnav: White Horse Hill, Oxfordshire SN7 7QJ (National Trust)

The village of Uffington is in the county of Oxfordshire today, but prior to the boundary changes of 1974 it was part of Berkshire, and therefore in the heart of Wessex. The village is probably best known as the home of the Uffington White Horse, thought to be the oldest white horse in Britain, but this is just one of the archaeological wonders the local landscape has to offer.

Uffington White Horse

The white horse lives next to Uffington Castle, an Iron Age bank and ditch style hill-fort which encloses around 8 acres of land and commands extensive views over the local countryside.

Directly below the white horse is a small chalk hillock that has a seemingly artificial flat top (visible at the upper left in the picture above). This hillock is known as Dragon Hill and is linked to the legend of King George and the dragon. The legend claims that the summit of the hill is where St George slew the dragon, and that the bare patch of chalk that can be seen is where the dragon's blood spilled (and hence no grass will now grow there). It has also been suggested that Dragon Hill may have been used for Iron Age rituals that were associated with the white horse.

Dragon Hill

Another interesting local feature, about a mile walk along the Ridgeway from Uffington Castle, is the Neolithic long barrow known as Wayland's Smithy. This tomb dates from around 3700 BC and is about 56m long by 13m wide. When the tomb was excavated in the 1960s it was found to contain the remains of 14 people, who seem to have been de-fleshed before burial.

Wayland's Smithy

The name of the tomb comes from the Saxons, who lived in the area around 4000 years after the tomb was built. They associated it with the Germanic god Wayland (also known as Wolund) who was a smith. The association of the tomb with Wayland the Smith gave rise to an interesting legend. Apparently if a traveller had a horse that had lost a shoe, leaving the horse at the tomb overnight, with a silver coin as payment, would result in the horse being re-shod by morning!

1.6 The Hell Stone

**Satnav: Near Hardy Monument, Dorset DT2 9HY (National Trust)
(park at monument and follow footpath to Hell Stone)**

The Hell Stone in Dorset is a Neolithic single-chambered tomb of the type known as a cromlech or dolmen. By the 19th century it had fallen into ruin, and was "restored" by a group of locals in what they thought was its correct form. Modern archaeologists disagree with this reconstruction, although there is no doubt the result is picturesque!

The Hell Stone

The Hell Stone is situated near a footpath running from the village of Portesham to the Hardy Monument – a 22-metre tall tower commemorating Admiral Hardy, who commanded Nelson's flagship HMS *Victory* at the Battle of Trafalgar. The Hardy Monument is now owned by the National Trust, and provides a convenient parking spot from which to reach both the Hell Stone and a Neolithic long barrow called "The Grey Mare and her Colts", about a mile to the west.

1.7 Roman Bath

Satnav: The Roman Baths, Bath, Somerset BA1 1LZ (admission charge)

The large town of Bath in Somerset gets its unusual name from the fact that, since Roman times, it has been home to a spa used for public bathing. The water bubbling up from the ground is naturally heated by geothermal energy, and widely believed to have therapeutic properties.

The Roman name for Bath was *Aquae Sulis* – from *aqua* meaning water and *Sulis*, the name of a local Celtic goddess. Even before the Romans arrived, the Celts had established a shrine to Sulis at the site. The Romans identified Sulis with their own goddess Minerva, and transformed the small shrine into a vast temple complex. The hot spring baths were just part of this complex, and their purpose was religious as much as it was recreational.

The Roman Baths

In the temple courtyards, animal sacrifices were carried out on a regular basis. The victim, typically a young calf, would have its throat slit on the altar of the goddess. The animal would then be disembowelled, allowing its entrails to be inspected by a soothsayer who would use them to foretell the future.

No fewer than 130 curse tablets have been unearthed at Bath, and many of them are on display in the museum there. People created these when they felt they had been wronged by someone, in the hope the goddess would take their side and wreak vengeance on their behalf. In June 2014, these tablets were added to the UNESCO Memory of the World register of outstanding documentary heritage; they are the oldest known prayers to a deity in Britain.

The world of Roman Britain was far from monotheistic, and other deities are represented in Bath besides Sulis-Minerva. A particularly popular one was Bacchus – the god of wine, drunkenness and debauchery!

Decapitated statue of Bacchus

1.8 Dorchester

Satnav: Dorchester Town Centre, Dorset DT1 1EE

Dorchester, the county town of Dorset, has a wealth of archaeological sites dating from different periods throughout history. One of the oldest can be found in the ignoble environment of an underground car park! Originally this was a wooden henge monument, built around 2000 BC. The post holes were discovered when the car park of Dorchester's branch of the Waitrose supermarket chain was being built – their positions are marked today by red circles painted on the floor.

Waitrose car park, with prehistoric post holes

A more visible reminder of prehistoric Dorchester can be seen at Maumbury Rings just off Weymouth Avenue. These imposing earthworks were originally built in the late Neolithic period, approximately 2500 BC. The site was still standing, though long disused, when the Romans invaded Britain in the 1st century AD. They decided to convert it to an amphitheatre, by removing earth from the centre of the rings and building up the surrounding bank. The result was one of the largest entertainment venues this side of the English Channel.

Another Roman relic in Dorchester is the Roman Town House, near Dorset County Hall. This was unearthed in the 1930s, when construction of the new office building was in progress. Fortunately its significance was recognised, and County Hall was built in a slightly different location, allowing the Roman ruin to remain visible to the public. Its most striking feature is its floor mosaics, which have been left in situ and covered over with a protective roof. This is one of the few places in the country where this has been done – Roman mosaics usually find themselves transferred into a museum.

Maumbury Rings

Roman Town House

Archaeology fans visiting Dorchester don't have to limit themselves to the local variety! The town also has two museums dedicated to more exotic archaeology. There is a Tutankhamun Exhibition on High West Street, featuring a recreation of the Egyptian pharaoh's tomb, from around 1300 BC, together with replicas of many of the treasures found there. A short distance away on High East Street is the Terracotta Warriors Museum, containing – again in replica form – a selection of the life-size clay figures that were buried along with the first Chinese emperor around 200 BC.

1.9 Glastonbury Abbey

Satnav: Glastonbury Abbey, Somerset BA6 9EL (admission charge)

Glastonbury is one of the most famous towns in Somerset. It is linked to countless legends revolving around Joseph of Arimathea, the Holy Grail and King Arthur. Some of these will be described later in this book, in the Chapter 6: *Weird Legends*, but Glastonbury has its share of Weird Archaeology, too.

Glastonbury Abbey was one of the first Christian monasteries in Britain, possibly dating as far back as Roman times. It was rebuilt several times during the Middle Ages, so its archaeology is complex to say the least. The first "archaeological dig" there occurred as long ago as 1191! That was when the monks, acting on cryptic hints in ancient documents, decided to look for the reputed tomb of King Arthur. They found it, too: a hollowed-out tree trunk, buried deep in the earth, containing skeletal remains. A lead cross bore the unambiguous inscription: *"Here lieth buried the famous King Arthur in the Isle of Avalon".*

Most people nowadays believe this was a cynical hoax, designed to attract pilgrims to the Abbey. But the idea that Arthur was buried at Glastonbury is not as ridiculous as it may sound. If he existed in real life, he wouldn't have been "King of Britain" as the legends claim, but simply a powerful local chieftain who lived a century or so after the Romans left. What more logical place to bury such a person than at the foremost religious establishment in the area?

A model of Glastonbury Abbey in its heyday

Weird Archaeology

By the time Glastonbury Abbey was dissolved in 1539, on the orders of King Henry VIII, it was the largest, wealthiest and most prestigious monastery in England. So prestigious, in fact, that the King was determined to make an example of it, ensuring that it was almost totally destroyed. As a result the Abbey was lost to history for 370 years, until the site was re-purchased by the Church of England in the early 20th century. That's when archaeological excavations were started in earnest.

The man in charge of the project, Frederick Bligh Bond, was an architect by profession, with no formal qualifications in archaeology. His main target was a part of the Abbey known as the Edgar Chapel. Prior to the excavations, only the existence and general location of the chapel were known – nothing about its shape, dimensions or exact position. Yet Bond seemed to know precisely where to dig – a fact that baffled his colleagues, who couldn't follow his methods at all.

In 1918, while the archaeological work was still continuing, Bond finally revealed his secret in a book called *The Gate of Remembrance*. It turned out that he had used a spiritualist medium, who had obtained information about the Abbey from long-dead monks using a technique known as automatic writing. The book records no less than sixteen specific pieces of information, which were not known at the time from any other source, but which were proved correct by excavations.

Spiritualism was far more popular a hundred years ago than it is today, but even in those days it was frowned on both by the Church, who thought it was the work of the Devil, and by academics, who thought it was the work of charlatans. So given that Bond was employed by the Church, and all his colleagues were academics, his fate was sealed. Not only did he lose his job, but he was ostracized by the authorities and his role in the excavations was airbrushed out of the official history. But the fact remains – he knew exactly where to dig for the Edgar Chapel.

Glastonbury Abbey with Edgar Chapel in the foreground

1.10 Kingston Lacy

Satnav: Kingston Lacy, Dorset BH21 4EA (National Trust)

Kingston Lacy is a large country house near Wimborne in Dorset, currently owned by the National Trust and open to the public. It was built by the Bankes family in the latter half of the 17th century, after their previous home – Corfe Castle – was reduced to ruins during the English Civil War.

One of the more interesting residents of Kingston Lacy was William John Bankes (1786 –1855), an explorer and adventurer who spent many years travelling around North Africa and the Middle East. Many of the artifacts he collected on his travels, particularly those from Egypt, can still be seen at Kingston Lacy. Unfortunately Bankes himself never got to enjoy his collection – he was banished from England in 1841 after being caught in a compromising position with a guardsman in London's Green Park!

Besides the extensive collection of Egyptian relics on show inside the house, the gardens at Kingston Lacy also contain some of Bankes' finds. Perhaps the best known of these is the 6.7 metre tall Philae Obelisk, which dates from the 2nd century BC and contains a bilingual inscription in Egyptian hieroglyphics and ancient Greek. More than a thousand years older still is the sarcophagus of Amenemope, also sitting there in an English country garden. Its former occupant (apparently no longer inside!) was the chief steward of the god Amun in the early part of the 19th Dynasty, around 1280 BC.

The Sarcophagus of Amenemope

2 Weird Buildings

This chapter describes some of the less well-known – not to mention weirder – aspects of Wessex architecture. The ten buildings are arranged thematically: first the ecclesiastical eccentricities of Wells Cathedral, the churches at Stockwood, Wilton and Wickham, and the chapels of St Aldhelm and Langport, and then the secular oddities of Castle Drogo, Lyme Regis Museum, Chesapeake Mill and Exeter's House that Moved.

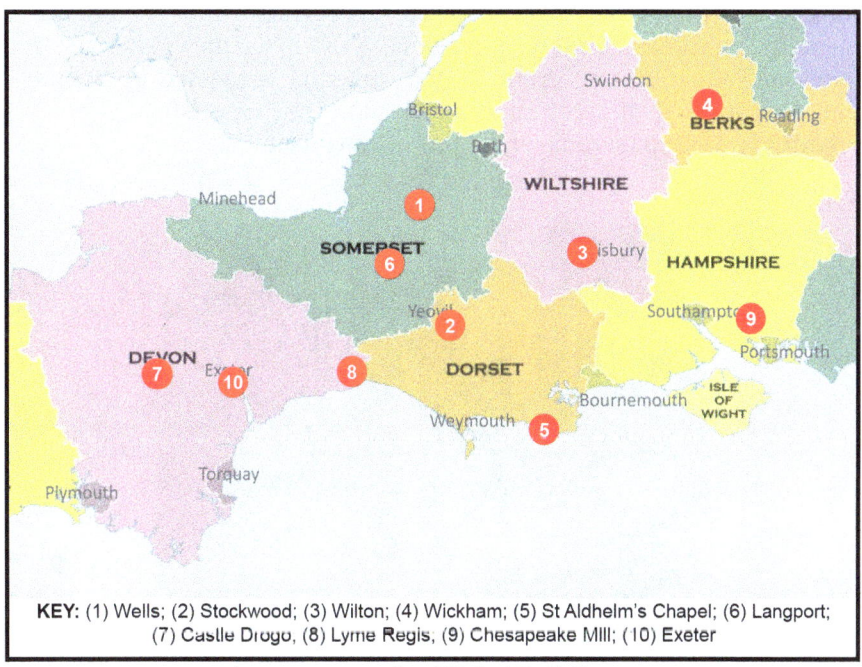

KEY: (1) Wells; (2) Stockwood; (3) Wilton; (4) Wickham; (5) St Aldhelm's Chapel; (6) Langport; (7) Castle Drogo; (8) Lyme Regis; (9) Chesapeake Mill; (10) Exeter

Locator map for Weird Buildings

2.1 Wells Cathedral

Satnav: Cathedral Green, Wells, Somerset BA5 2UE

With a population of little more than 10,000, Wells in Somerset is the smallest city in England. What makes it a city, rather than a medium-sized town, is the presence of St Andrew's cathedral, built between the 12th and 15th centuries.

Wells Cathedral is unusual amongst English cathedrals in the sheer quantity of stone sculpture it contains – both on the inside and the outside. The entire west front of the cathedral is covered in statues – more so even than most continental cathedrals – producing what is essentially a vast panorama of the Day of Judgment.

The west front of Wells Cathedral

Inside the cathedral, the arches supporting the tower have a peculiar scissor-like shape. Originally only the conventional lower halves of these arches were present, but when the tower was added in 1338 the whole building began to subside and the walls cracked. The upper, inverted arches were added as a precautionary measure at that time... and they seem to have done the trick, because the tower is still standing!

Weird Buildings

One of the inverted arches

Despite being such a sacred place, many of the stone carvings inside the cathedral are far from sacred in their subject-matter. This is particularly true of the small carvings, called "capitals", at the top of each column. One of the best known of these shows a man with an unhappy expression poking a finger in his mouth as if he has toothache. Another, reproduced below, depicts a farmer hitting a would-be thief over the head with a stick!

One of the Wells capitals

2.2 Stockwood Church

Satnav: Stockwood, Dorset DT2 0NG

The small village of Stockwood in Dorset lies just off the main A37 road between Dorchester and Yeovil. Its tiny church, dedicated to St Edwold, is one of the smallest in the country – just 9 metres long by 4 metres wide. The present building dates from the 15th century, with a porch and bell turret added in the 17th century. There may, however, have been an earlier church on the same site with the same rather obscure dedication: St Edwold was a local hermit who lived in the 9th century.

Stockwood church

The church is no longer in use, although it is maintained in good condition by the Churches Conservation Trust and is open to the public. There are no parking facilities in the immediate vicinity of the church; visitors are recommended to find a safe place to park by the side of the road and approach on foot.

2.3 Wilton Church

Satnav: West Street, Wilton, Wiltshire SP2 0DL

The Wiltshire town of Wilton, which is virtually synonymous with English carpet manufacture, is not the sort of place you would expect to find a magnificently ornate Italian church. But that is exactly what Wilton has.

The edifice in question is the church of St Mary and St Nicholas, which was built on West Street between 1841 and 1844, as a replacement for the town's 15th century church of St Mary's.

The new church was commissioned by Lord Herbert of Lea with support from his mother, the Dowager Countess of Pembroke, who was of Russian descent. Lord Herbert had a passion for Italian architecture, as a result of which the architects created the church in a mock Romanesque style, with additional Byzantine embellishments. It is possible the church was built in imitation of a specific basilica in Lombardy, Italy.

Wilton church

One of the most striking features of this impressive building is its 105 foot high campanile, which is connected to the church by a short cloister adorned with carved columns. The church also boasts crafted items that were imported from Europe to be incorporated into the building, such as marble columns from the 2nd century BC Temple of Venus at Porto Venere, and 12th and 13th century stained glass from France. The church even contains a 17th century engraved metal chest from Germany.

Not all of the church's adornments are from exotic locales however; the church bells were recycled from those melted down from the old St Mary's church.

Another unusual feature of the church is its alignment. It lies on a north-east to south-west axis, as opposed to the more traditional east-west alignment.

Carved columns in the cloister

2.4 Wickham Church

Satnav: St Swithun's church, Wickham, Berkshire RG20 8HD

The village of Wickham lies about five miles north-west of Newbury in Berkshire. The local church, dedicated to St Swithun, is notable because its tower dates from the Saxon era, making it one of the oldest in the country. The church is located near the site of an ancient Roman camp, and recycled Roman tiles and columns can be seen incorporated in to the tower's construction. It is thought to have been built originally as a free-standing watch tower, with access to the first floor provided by a ladder that could be pulled up when the need arose. The main body of the church would have been a later addition to the tower.

St Swithun's church

The church's biggest oddity, however, lies in the interior. As you enter the nave of the church, carved angels can be seen decorating the roof beams – a fairly standard type of decoration for a church. However, when you move into the north aisle, which houses the church's organ, the roof beams are unusually decorated by eight large golden elephants.

It seems that between 1845 and 1849 the church underwent an extensive refurbishment in which the nave, chancel and north and south aisles were largely rebuilt. The person responsible for this work was a William Nicholson, and it was during a visit to an exhibition in Paris that he is said to have impulsively bought four papier maché elephants to decorate the church. Needing four more elephants to complete the task, Nicholson apparently had another four specially commissioned to finish the new look of the north aisle.

Some of Wickham's golden elephants

2.5 St Aldhelm's Chapel

**Satnav: St Aldhelm's Head, Worth Matravers, Dorset BH19 3LQ
(park in village and follow footpath to chapel)**

St Aldhelm's Chapel resides inside a low circular earthwork on St Aldhelm's Head near Worth Matravers in Dorset. The building is believed to date from the Norman period, although there is no written record of it as a chapel before the 13th century. Unusually for a chapel it is square (25 feet by 25 feet), rather than rectangular, and the interior is dominated by a massive central column. Another strange feature of the chapel is its isolated location: around 1.5 miles from Worth Matravers, with no archaeological evidence of any historic settlements closer to the chapel.

St Aldhelm's Chapel

Due to its peculiar features, St Aldhelm's Chapel has become known locally as "the Devil's chapel". It is possible the building was not designed as a chapel at all, but for some other purpose. One suggestion is that it was originally built as a coastal watchtower for Corfe Castle, four miles to the north. The fact is, however, that no-one knows for sure when the chapel was built, by whom or for what purpose!

2.6 The Hanging Chapel

Satnav: The Hill, Langport, Somerset TA10 9PU

One of the more unusual sights in the small Somerset town of Langport is the so-called Hanging Chapel. This dates from the 13th century, and consists of a massive stone archway with a small chapel perched on top. The arch is all that remains of the mediaeval gateway into what at that time was a walled town.

Despite its precarious position, the Hanging Chapel has remained intact for over 700 years. However, it is a long time since it was used as a chapel. After the Protestant Reformation in the 16th century it served as the Town Hall, and later a courthouse, before becoming the local Masonic Lodge in 1891 – a role it retains to this day.

The Hanging Chapel

2.7 Castle Drogo

Satnav: Castle Drogo, Devon EX6 6PB (National Trust)

The word "castle" is inextricably linked in the minds of most people with the Middle Ages. But Castle Drogo, on the northern edge of Dartmoor in Devon, was built entirely in the 20th century. It was commissioned as a private home by Julius Drewe, who made his fortune from the Home and Colonial Stores, one of Britain's first nationwide supermarket chains. The architect he selected was Sir Edwin Lutyens, who is probably most famous as the designer of the Cenotaph in Whitehall.

Castle Drogo gets is strange-sounding name from a Norman baron named Drogo de Teigne, whom Julius Drewe believed to be an ancestor of his. Drogo de Teigne's estate was at a place named Drewsteignton, which is close to the site Drewe chose for Castle Drogo. Work on the castle began in 1911, but the building wasn't completed until 1930, just a year before Drewe's death.

The castle had to be reduced in scale from Drewe's original vision, but it is still one of the largest private homes built in the 20th century. It is constructed entirely of Dartmoor granite, in a style that mingles the mediaeval gothic tradition with 20th century brutalism. It remains the last castle to be built in England, and the only one to have had electrical fittings designed in from the start. The castle's power comes from its own hydroelectric turbines on the nearby river Teign.

Castle Drogo

2.8 Lyme Regis Museum

Satnav: Bridge Street, Lyme Regis, Dorset DT7 3QA (admission charge)

Lyme Regis is a small town on the Dorset coast which is chiefly famous for the multitude of Jurassic-period fossils that can be found in its cliffs. Visitors have been coming from far and wide to see fossils – either in situ or in local exhibitions – since the beginning of the 19th century. The town's best known fossil collector was Mary Anning, who discovered the first ichthyosaur skeleton at the age of 12 in 1811. She went on to run her own fossil-selling business, in a shop on the site of the present-day Lyme Regis Museum. Mary's shop was so packed full of curiosities that it was almost a museum itself – it is said to have attracted visitors that included the crowned heads of Europe!

In the last decade of the 19th century, the mayor of Lyme Regis, Thomas Philpot, organized a major exhibition of fossils and other curiosities at the Guildhall. This was so well attended that Philpot decided to commission Lyme's very own purpose-built museum – an astonishing undertaking for a town of just 2000 inhabitants.

Lyme Regis Museum

Weird Buildings

The Museum was completed in 1901, and turned out to be just as idiosyncratic as its intended contents. It was designed by a rather eccentric local architect named George Vialls, who seems to have had some difficulty deciding what style to use for the building. It ended up as a bizarre mixture of Dutch renaissance, Jacobean and Art Nouveau, giving it a distinctly folly-like appearance. The architect also neglected to design in any storage space, administrative offices or toilet facilities! Nevertheless, the Museum has an enviable location, perched right on the sea wall.

Next door to Lyme Regis Museum is the town's Guildhall, which was constructed in the 19th century on the site of a former courthouse. An unusual relic of the latter can still be seen today, in the form of the doorway to what used to be the court's lock-up!

The door to the old lock-up

2.9 Chesapeake Mill

Satnav: Bridge Street, Wickham, Hampshire PO17 5JH

The village of Wickham in Hampshire is home to a rather unusual building, known as the Chesapeake Mill. This old watermill was built in 1820 and worked as a commercial watermill until 1976. Since then it has served as an antiques and craft shop. Interestingly, however, the history of the Chesapeake Mill really started way back on the 2nd December 1799, when the USS *Chesapeake* was launched from the Gosport Navy Yard in Norfolk, Virginia.

The Chesapeake Mill

The *Chesapeake* was a wooden three-masted heavy frigate of the United States Navy, rated at 38 guns. Her military career included service in the quasi-war against France (1798 – 1800), the First Barbary War against the Muslim Barbary States of Northwest Africa (1801 – 1805) and finally the "War of 1812" between the United States and the United Kingdom.

In December 1812 the USS *Chesapeake* commenced her first patrol of the War of 1812. During this patrol she was responsible for the capture of five British merchant vessels and the re-capture of an American vessel from

British privateers. She completed this patrol by returning to Boston on the 9th April 1813 where she underwent a refit and a change of Commanding Officer. Whilst the *Chesapeake* was refitting in Boston, the British 38-gun frigate HMS *Shannon* arrived at Boston and commenced a blockade of the port.

By the 1st June 1813, the USS *Chesapeake* was again ready to put to sea, so she sailed out of Boston to challenge HMS *Shannon*'s blockade of the port. The ships were evenly matched, with the two vessels being of comparable size and armament. After a brief exchange of cannon fire, HMS *Shannon* scored the first hit and the two vessels were soon alongside each other. The British ship concentrated her fire on the American gun crews, killing many of them. The *Chesapeake* was finally disabled by cannon fire which destroyed her wheel, leaving her unable to manoeuvre. The entire battle only lasted around 11 minutes, at the end of which the British had boarded the *Chesapeake* and subdued the remaining crew.

The captured frigate was eventually repaired by the Royal Navy and put back into service as HMS *Chesapeake*. She continued to serve until 1819, when she was sold to a timber merchant who broke up the vessel and sold the timbers to a local miller – who used them in the construction of the Chesapeake Mill!

HMS Shannon versus USS Chesapeake (public domain image)

2.10 The House that Moved

Satnav: West Street, Exeter, Devon EX1 1BA

One of the oldest buildings in Exeter is the timber-framed Merchant House, which originally stood on Edmund Street. It may date from as long ago as the 14th century, although more conservative estimates put the date of construction around 1450. More than 500 years later, its existence came under threat when Exeter City Council decided to build a new road through the site. They were stopped in the nick of time by archaeologists who recognized the building's historical significance.

The solution they came up with was a novel one. The 21-tonne house was strengthened with a further 10 tonnes of wooden scaffolding, wheels were attached to each corner and the house was jacked up onto iron rails. Then, over a period of five days in December 1961, it was gently moved 70 metres to its present location at the end of West Street. Despite its top-heavy construction, the house survived its ordeal and it is now home to a shop selling wedding gowns!

The House that Moved

3 Weird Constructions

There's more to the weird architecture of Wessex than buildings designed to be lived in – there are engineering works and military defences, and even follies with no apparent purpose at all. The ten items in this chapter are arranged roughly chronologically, from Maud Heath's 15th century causeway and the 17th century Combe Gibbet, through the 18th century follies of Stourhead, Horton and Farley Mount, to the 19th century defences around Portsmouth, the 20th century industrial archaeology of the New Forest, Kilve and Kimmeridge, and finally the modern-day "follies" of Solstice Park.

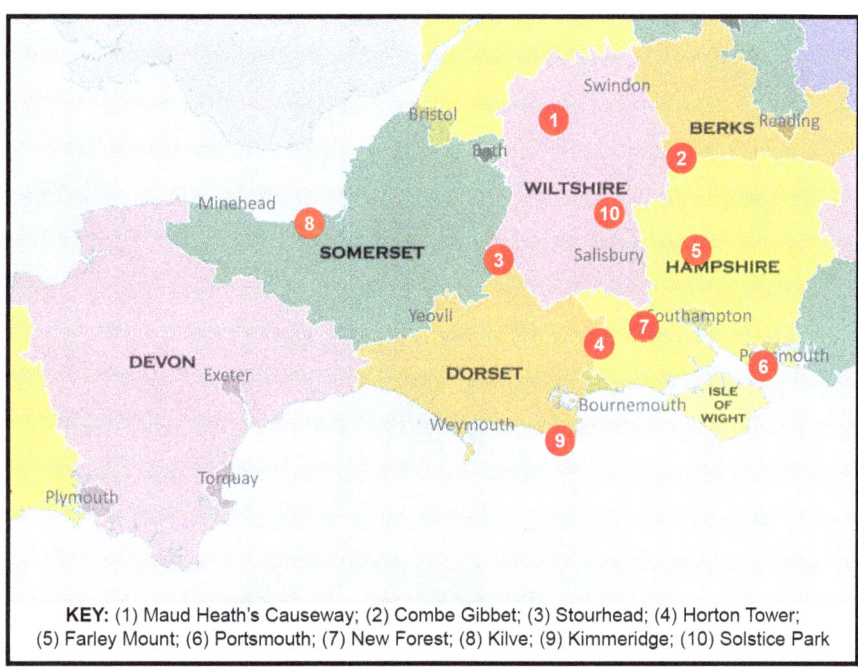

KEY: (1) Maud Heath's Causeway; (2) Combe Gibbet; (3) Stourhead; (4) Horton Tower; (5) Farley Mount; (6) Portsmouth; (7) New Forest; (8) Kilve; (9) Kimmeridge; (10) Solstice Park

Locator map for Weird Constructions

3.1 Maud Heath's Causeway

Satnav: Near Langley Burrell, Wiltshire SN15 4LL

On Wick Hill, near the village of Bremhill in Wiltshire, stands a monument erected in 1838 to a lady called Maud Heath. The monument consists of a plinth capped off by the statue of a lady in a bonnet. The base of the plinth bears the inscription:

> *Thou who dost pause on this aerial height*
> *Where Maud Heath's Pathway*
> *   winds in shade and light*
> *Christian wayfarer in a world of strife*
> *Be still and consider the Path of Life.*

The monument to Maud Heath on Wick Hill

It seems that Maud Heath was a local land owner in the 15th Century, who held properties in both Langley Burrell and Chippenham. She is remembered locally mainly for the folly she commissioned – Maud Heath's Causeway.

Maud was apparently concerned that the local people from the villages of Bremhill, Foxham, Tytherton and Langley Burrell were having difficulties

Weird Constructions

getting from their villages to the market in Chippenham, as they had to cross the marshy River Avon floodplain – a route that Maud had seemingly used for most of her life herself. So in response to her concern, in June 1474 (the year of her death) Maud provided a trust with the finance to enable a 4.5 mile cobble causeway to be built from Wick in Bremhill to Chippenham. This causeway was further improved by the trust in 1811 when the part of the causeway that crossed the River Avon was updated to include a bridge made up of 64 small brick arches. These brick arches can still be seen today as they raise the footpath up above the level of the local road that follows the route of the causeway - a road still shown on Ordnance Survey maps today as "Maud Heath's Causeway".

Maud Heath's Causeway

3.2 The Combe Gibbet

Satnav: Inkpen Hill, near Combe, Berkshire RG17 9EL (approx)

On the Test Way footpath near the village of Combe in Berkshire, the ominous shape of a gibbet can be seen on top of Inkpen Hill... or to be pedantic, on top of a Bronze Age long barrow on the summit of the hill. The original gibbet was erected in this prominent location in 1676 in order to display the bodies of two convicted murderers, as a deterrent to anyone else contemplating such a crime.

The murderers in question were a pair of lovers, George Broomham and Dorothy Newman. Broomham was married with a son while Newman was a widow when they commenced their illicit relationship. Accounts vary, but it appears that at some point they murdered Broomham's wife and son – probably because divorce was practically impossible at that time. Unluckily for them they were witnessed in the act, and put on trial in Winchester, where they were found guilty of murder.

The pair were hanged in public three days later, after which the bodies were moved to Inkpen Hill where they were displayed on the gibbet. The original gibbet is long gone – the one that can be seen today, dating from 1992, is the latest in a long line of replicas.

The Combe Gibbet

3.3 The Temples of Stourhead

Satnav: Stourton, Wiltshire BA12 6QF (National Trust)

When Henry Hoare II inherited the Stourhead estate on the death of his mother in 1741, he had just returned from a grand tour of Europe. Deeply impressed by the classical architecture he had seen on the continent, with its connections to ancient Greek and Roman mythology, he was determined to recreate as much of it as possible at Stourhead. The result is probably the most highbrow garden in England!

Stourhead lies in the village of Stourton in Wiltshire, close to the border with Somerset. The estate is now owned by the National Trust, which means that it's regularly open to the public – despite the stern Latin injunction *procul este profani* ("Begone, outsiders") found on one of its temples!

View of Stourhead showing the Pantheon

The largest of Stourhead's temples is the Pantheon, which was built in 1753 to a design by the architect Henry Flitcroft. As the name suggests this is a kind of scaled-down replica of the Pantheon in Rome – albeit with a much more picturesque setting. In literal terms a pantheon is a temple to "all the gods", but at Stourhead it's more a case of "all the classical-looking statues Henry Hoare could get his hands on". In pride of place at the centre is the Graeco-Roman hero Hercules, flanked by the Roman goddesses Diana, Flora and Ceres, the Greek hero Meleager, the Egyptian goddess Isis and even the Christian heroine St Susanna.

Flitcroft also designed Stourhead's two other classical-style temples. The first, built in 1743, was dedicated to the goddess Flora, and the other, dating from 1765, to the god Apollo. The latter is based on a circular temple found at Baalbek in Lebanon.

The Temple of Apollo

Not all the constructions at Stourhead are classical in form. The Grotto, dating from 1748, is a kind of artificial cave, housing the statue of an unnamed "river god". It also has a statue of Ariadne, from Greek mythology, as seen in the photograph below.

The Grotto with statue of Ariadne

Weird Constructions

On another part of the Stourhead estate, also owned by the National Trust, is the huge folly known as King Alfred's Tower. Like Stourhead's temples, this was commissioned by Henry Hoare II and designed by Henry Flitcroft. The tower stands 49 metres high, and is essentially three round towers connected to form a single triangular tower, comprised of over a million bricks. The entrance to the tower is guarded by a three metre high statue of King Alfred the Great.

The tower is believed to stand near the spot where King Alfred rallied his troops prior to the Battle of Edington in 878 AD. The battle proved to be Alfred's greatest victory, in which Guthrum's "Great Viking Army", which had been terrorising the countryside, was finally defeated.

King Alfred's Tower

3.4 Horton Tower

Satnav: Horton, Dorset BH21 7EP (approx)

The folly known as Horton Tower can be found near the village of Horton in Dorset. It was built in 1750 by the lord of Horton Manor, Humphrey Sturt, who was an architect and also an MP for Dorset. The exact reason why Sturt built the tower is unclear. The practice of folly building was popular in the 18th and 19th centuries, and they were often built purely to be admired as eye-catching constructions rather than having any practical function. It is possible however that Horton Tower did serve some practical purpose, possibly as an observatory for star gazing, or for watching nearby hunts.

Horton Tower

The brick tower has a triangular footprint with round turrets at each corner. It rises up to a height of 140 feet (43 metres), which supposedly made it the tallest non-religious building in England at the time of its construction. The tower's shape and style is similar to that of King Alfred's Tower at Stourhead (see previous item), which was built a few years later and is slightly larger at 161 feet (49 metres) in height – possibly a deliberate act of one-upmanship!

The village of Horton is noteworthy for another reason, in that it was the location where the Duke of Monmouth was captured after his defeat at the Battle of Sedgemoor in 1685 (see Chapter 4: *Weird History*). The Duke is said to have hidden in a ditch under an ash tree in Horton disguised as a shepherd. Sadly for him his hiding place was discovered by a local and he was soon captured, and then beheaded at Tower Hill in London a week later.

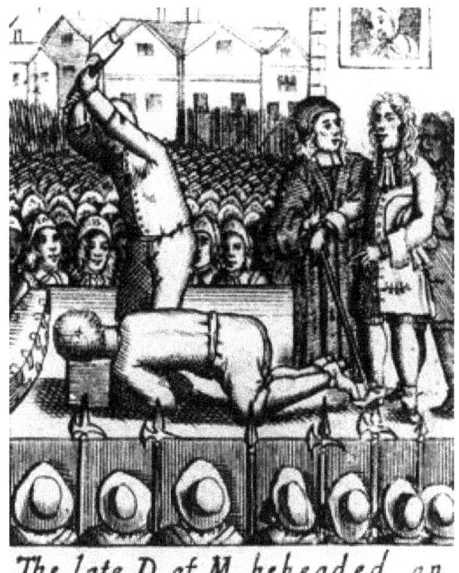

Execution of the Duke of Monmouth (public domain image)

3.5 Farley Mount

Satnav: Farley Mount Country Park, Hampshire SO22 5QS (approx)

A few miles west of Winchester in Hampshire is Farley Mount Country Park, which is home to a striking monument dedicated to a horse. Farley Mount itself is a hill, on top of which stands an impressive-looking folly. This was built in memory of a horse named "Beware Chalk Pit", which is reportedly buried beneath the monument.

The monument on Farley Mount

The horse in question was owned by one Paulet St John Esquire. It is said that whilst out fox hunting in September 1733, the horse and rider fell into a twenty-five foot deep chalk pit. Both man and horse survived this calamity, and in October of the following year this "lucky" horse was entered into the Hunters Plate on Worthy Downs under the name of "Beware Chalk Pit". The horse won the race, and this victory is presumably the reason why the owner created such a magnificent folly in honour of the animal.

Weird Constructions

3.6 Portsmouth Sea Forts

Satnav: Southsea seafront, Portsmouth, Hampshire PO5 3PA

In 1859 the Prime Minister of the day, Lord Palmerston, set up a Royal Commission to assess the country's ability to defend itself against a French invasion. The Commission concluded that Britain's present defences were inadequate to the task, and recommended a whole new series of fortifications all around the English coast. These are collectively referred to as Palmerston Forts, or less politely as Palmerston's Follies – since by the time they were finished, France had long since ceased to pose any threat of invasion.

Brean Down Fort in Somerset, described later in this book in Chapter 8: *Weird Science*, was one of Palmerston's follies, as was the Verne Citadel on Portland, described in Chapter 9: *Weird Secrets*. But perhaps the best known and most extensive array of Palmerston Forts can be found around Portsmouth in Hampshire.

Four of the Portsmouth forts were constructed in the sea itself. Most easily visible from the land is Spitbank Fort, just over a kilometre from the seafront at Southsea. This is approximately 50 metres in diameter, and built from granite, iron and concrete. In its heyday in the 19th century it was armed with 12-inch calibre breech-loading guns, which remained in service until after the First World War. Today it is a luxury hotel and entertainment venue!

Spitbank Fort

A more traditional fortification is Southsea Castle, on the mainland opposite Spitbank Fort. This was originally built in the 16th century on the orders of King Henry VIII. It was completed in 1544, just a year before the battle of the Solent which saw the sinking of Henry's flagship, the *Mary Rose* (now on display in its own purpose-built museum in Portsmouth's historic dockyard). Following Lord Palmerston's Royal Commission, Southsea Castle was rearmed and refurbished, becoming the central command post for the new Palmerston forts.

Southsea Castle

The remains of the *Mary Rose*

Weird Constructions

3.7 The Portuguese Fireplace

Satnav: Near Lyndhurst, Hampshire SO43 7GR (approx)

In the New Forest in Hampshire between the village of Emery Down and the Bolderwood Deer Sanctuary, close to Millyford Bridge, there is a stone fireplace sitting on a patch of grass beside the road. The "Portuguese Fireplace", as it is known, serves as an unusual kind of war memorial to honour the role played by foreign military units stationed in the New Forest during the First World War.

By 1916, most of the skilled local foresters were away fighting the war, so foreign military manpower was required to plug the shortfall. The Canadian Forestry Corps sent men and equipment to the UK, and the lumber camp set up in the New Forest became a significant settlement, housing around 200 Canadians and 150 Portuguese labourers. The buildings were temporary, however, and the stone fireplace of the camp's cookhouse is all that remains today.

The Portuguese Fireplace

3.8 Kilve Oil Retort

Satnav: Kilve Beach, Somerset TA5 1EG (approx)

The village of Kilve in Somerset is located near the Bristol Channel, about half-way between the resort towns of Minehead and Burnham-on-Sea. But Kilve's most unusual sight is not connected with the tourist industry but with the oil industry.

In 1916 it was discovered that the shale beds of Kilve beach and the surrounding coast were rich in oil deposits. The Shaline Company was formed in 1924 to take advantage of this discovery, and a brick-built oil retort house was erected at that time. It is believed to be the first building ever constructed for the extraction of oil from shale.

For a brief period there promised to be an "oil boom" in North Somerset. Sadly however, the enterprise never really got off the ground, as the process was found to be too costly to make it profitable. Nevertheless, the oil retort building is still standing to this day.

As can be seen from the photograph, it appears at first sight that there is still smoke coming from the building's chimney. On closer inspection, however, it is not smoke but a small shrub that is growing from the chimney. The prevailing wind has had the same effect on the foliage as it would have on real smoke!

The Kilve oil retort

3.9 Kimmeridge Oil Well

Satnav: Kimmeridge Bay, Dorset BH20 5PF (approx)

It's a little known fact that Dorset has its own small-scale oil industry. Just to the west of Kimmeridge Bay there is a "nodding donkey" extracting oil from this part of the Jurassic Coast. Oil operations have been ongoing here since 1935, when people began to search for the source of small seepages of oil that are seen in various locations around the Dorset coast.

The Kimmeridge Nodding Donkey

Between 1958 and 1980 six wells were drilled in Kimmeridge Bay, although only one of these wells (known as K1) exposed worthwhile reserves of oil and gas seeping from the rocks around 500 meters below the coast. Following this discovery, oil extraction was soon set up and the "nodding donkey" at the Kimmeridge K1 site has been pumping non-stop since 1961, giving it the honour of being the oldest working oil well in the UK. The K1 pump currently draws oil from 350 metres below sea level, and at its peak it was producing 350 barrels of oil per day. These days its output has been reduced to around 80 to 65 barrels per day.

The Kimmeridge K1 well is now part of the larger Wytch Farm oil field and processing facility that extracts and processes oil from a number of locations in the Purbeck Region. The Wytch Farm oil field is the largest onshore oil field in Western Europe – yet many people who live in Dorset are blissfully unaware that black gold is being extracted from beneath their feet!

3.10 Solstice Park

Satnav: Solstice Park, Wiltshire SP4 7SQ

Solstice Park can be found on the A303 a few miles east of Stonehenge, near Amesbury in Wiltshire. At first sight it is a typical roadside service area which is home to the usual amenities such as a petrol station, hotel and fast food restaurants. The thing that makes Solstice Park stand out from the crowd, however, is the resident sculptures that have been added to the service area over the years.

Six of these creations are the result of a six-year community project that ran from 2007 to 2013. The project saw a local sculptress and a local business work together to create the artworks, which were commissioned by the Salisbury International Arts Festival. The six sculptures are:

- The Dragonfly: Unveiled on the 11th June 2007, this sculpture of a Dragonfly recycles parts of a Gazelle helicopter. Whilst the sculpture is intended to resemble a Dragonfly, from certain angles it also looks like a duck in flight.

The Dragonfly

- The Mallow: Unveiled on the 24th June 2007, the 8m tall sculpture named The Mallow was inspired by a flower (the Common Mallow) which once grew extensively on the chalk-land of Solstice Park. The sculpture features the nose-cone of a Beagle Bulldog airplane at its centre, and also includes materials that are more usually used in the construction of road signs.

Weird Constructions

- The Avon: Unveiled on the 10th September 2009, The Avon aims to represent the River Avon as it meanders from Amesbury to Salisbury. The sculpture consists of 105 vertical steel poles which undulate over a distance of 30 metres. The steel poles range in height from 90 cm to 2 metres and are set into a bed of napped flint which is inset with blue solar-powered road studs, to represent sparkling water.

- The White Horse: Unveiled on the 21st September 2010, The White Horse is a life-sized sculpture that uses bent steel tubing and floating plates of powdercoated steel to depict a thoroughbred mare. The shape of the horse is based on the Uffington White Horse (described in Chapter 1, *Weird Archaeology*).

The White Horse

- The Red Kite: Unveiled on the 4th October 2011, The Red Kite was built using welded and powder-coated steel tubing and perforated steel plates. The aim of the sculpture is to celebrating Red Kites, which are beginning to make a come back into the local countryside.

The Red Kite

- Bladehenge: Unveiled on the 11th March 2013, Bladehenge was the final sculpture in the series of six. It was supposedly inspired by the aeronautical forms of propellers and turbines, and features three twisted steel monoliths which resemble nearby Stonehenge.

Solstice Park is also home to a huge sculpture known as The Ancestor, which was created by a local pair of artists under a different initiative. The Ancestor is a 6.7m tall sculpture weighing around 6 tonnes. It was constructed out of thousands of hand-cut pieces of steel which were welded to a steel frame, over a period of nine months. The Ancestor is not a permanent fixture at Solstice Park – he sometimes takes the trip to Stonehenge to welcome in the Summer Solstice.

The Ancestor

4 Weird History

There are many reminders – for those who care to look – of the weirder events in the long history of Wessex. The ten items in this chapter are arranged chronologically, from mediaeval murders in Harewood Forest and the New Forest, and the royal adventures of England's forgotten queen Matilda and boy-king Edward VI, through the turmoil of the Civil War and Monmouth Rebellion to the Napoleonic Wars and the Industrial Age of the 19th century.

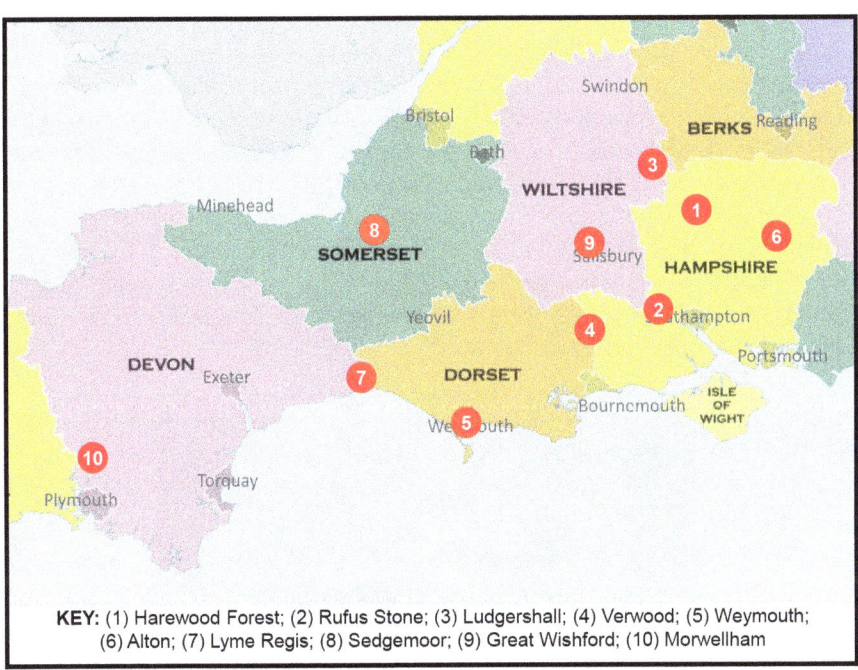

Locator map for Weird History

4.1 Dead Man's Plack

Satnav: Harewood Forest, Hampshire SP11 6LS (approx)

Just outside Andover in Hampshire, hidden inside Harewood Forest near Longparish, a 19th century stone cross can be found. The cross – known as "Dead Man's Plack" (*sic*) was erected in 1825 by Lieutenant Colonel William Iremonger. The inscription on the cross commemorates an event that was believed to have occurred within Harewood Forest in 963 AD, perhaps even at the very location of the cross.

As the story goes, King Edgar, a great grandson of Alfred the Great, was looking for a Queen. The King, known as "Edgar the Peaceful", had heard about the beauty of a lady called Elfrida. He dispatched his adviser Earl Athelwold of Wherwell to check if the claims of Elfrida's beauty were true. If they were, the Earl was ordered to present the King's offer of marriage. However, after meeting Elfrida, Athelwold (presumably enraptured by her beauty) decided to marry her himself and to report to the King that she was not suitable for him to marry. King Edgar, not being easily duped, found out about the deception and arranged for Athelwold to be killed during a hunt in Harewood Forest.

Dead Man's Plack

Weird History

4.2 The Rufus Stone

Satnav: The New Forest, Hampshire SO43 7HD (approx)

The Rufus Stone is a small monument which can be found in the New Forest National Park between the village of Brook and the A31 trunk road, near to the Sir Walter Tyrrell pub. The stone commemorates the death of William II of England, known as William Rufus.

The Rufus Stone

William Rufus was the third of the four sons of England's first Norman king, William the Conqueror; his two older brothers were Robert and Richard, while his younger brother was Henry. Richard was killed in 1075 whilst hunting in the New Forest, leaving William as the second oldest. When William I died in September 1087, the eldest son Robert became Duke of Normandy while William II became King of England.

The commonly accepted account of William Rufus's death is that he came to grief in a hunting accident in the New Forest, just as his older brother Richard had. On the 2nd August 1100, the king and a man named Walter Tyrell (or Tirel) became separated from the rest of the hunting party, which included William's younger brother Henry. Tyrell is supposed to have shot an arrow at a stag, but the arrow deflected off an oak tree and struck William in the chest, killing him instantly. Tyrell fled the scene and escaped to France before he could be questioned about what had happened. Meanwhile, the younger brother Henry wasted no time in getting himself crowned king just a few days later.

4.3 Ludgershall Castle

Satnav: Ludgershall Castle, Wiltshire SP11 9QT (English Heritage)

Ludgershall today is an unremarkable army town on the Wiltshire/Hampshire border, but it has a recorded history that stretches back to the Domesday Book (1086) and beyond. At that time the town was referred to as Litlegarsele, which apparently translates to "small grazing area".

Ludgershall boasts its own castle, although today only a series of earthworks and a ruin remain. Ludgershall Castle is believed to have been built in the late 11th century by Edward of Salisbury, becoming a royal property around 1100. Over the years the defences were improved, and in 1210 King John renovated the castle and adopted it as a hunting lodge. This hunting lodge was subsequently used by his son, Henry III. The castle remained in use as a hunting lodge and was frequented by royal visitors until it eventually fell into disrepair in the 15th century.

Ludgershall Castle

Ludgershall Castle also played a role in the tale of England's "forgotten" queen, the Empress Matilda. She was the legitimate heir to the throne when Henry I died in 1135, at which time she was married to a

Weird History

Frenchman, Geoffrey Plantagenet (her title of "Empress" stemmed from her previous marriage). Matilda found herself in a power struggle for the English crown with her cousin Stephen of Blois, and the resulting civil war, known as the "Anarchy", tore the country in two until Stephen's death in 1154.

In September 1141, King Stephen's army defeated Matilda's forces who were besieging them at Winchester. Following this rout, Matilda fled to Gloucester – and en-route she sought refuge at Ludgershall Castle. Matilda had the last laugh, however, because after Stephen's death the crown passed to her son, Henry II, this beginning the Plantagenet dynasty that ruled England for over three hundred years.

The castle ruins

4.4 The Remedy Oak

Satnav: Woodlands, near Verwood, Dorset BH21 8NG (approx)

In the hamlet of Woodlands, just off of the B3081 near Verwood in Dorset, there is an old hollowed-out oak tree known locally as the Remedy Oak. The tree is estimated to be around 800 years old and a small metal plaque near its base bears the following cryptic inscription:

> *According to tradition King Edward VI sat beneath this tree and touched for King's evil.*

The young King Edward VI is said to have stopped by this tree whilst out hunting one day in the summer of 1552. At that time most people believed that an anointed king possessed special powers to cure the sick. So a gaggle of locals appeared and asked the king to touch them to cure their ills!

The phrase "King's evil" on the plaque refers to a specific disease known as scrofula, and there was a longstanding belief that the "royal touch" could cure this disease. Apparently, however, Edward VI himself suffered from scrofula and was unable to cure himself of it. He died – possibly from this or a related disease – the following year, 1553.

The Remedy Oak

4.5 Weymouth's Cannonball

Satnav: Weymouth town centre, Dorset DT4 8AY

The seaside town of Weymouth in Dorset was one of England's first really fashionable holiday destinations, after King George III used it as his summer retreat in the late 18th and early 19th centuries. But the history of the town goes back much further than that – it is even said to be the place where the Black Death entered the country from France in June 1348.

Weymouth seafront, centred on George III's residence

One of Weymouth's most intriguing historical oddities can be seen on Maiden Street, on a building which today is a public convenience. When looking at this building, if you happen to glance upwards, you may notice what appears to be a cannonball lodged in the wall.

During the English Civil War in the 1640s, there was a plot by Royalist sympathisers, loyal to King Charles I, known as the Crabchurch Conspiracy. The ultimate aim of the plot was to secure a port, Weymouth, to allow the King to land a force of French soldiers and bolster his chances of winning the war. This attempt to secure a port led to some extensive fighting in the town, with a force of circa 1000 Roundheads pitched against a force of circa 6000 Royalists. It is commonly believed that the cannonball found its way into the wall during this battle.

The Weymouth Cannonball

4.6 The Battle of Alton

Satnav: Alton, Hampshire, GU34 2BU

The church of St Lawrence in Alton, Hampshire, still shows the scars of its involvement in an English Civil War battle. The Battle of Alton occurred on the 13th December 1643 when Parliamentarian forces under Sir William Waller undertook a surprise attack on Royalist infantry and cavalry units commanded by the Earl of Crawford.

Alton church

Waller's Parliamentarian forces commenced their attack on Alton at dawn. As the Parliamentarians approached, the Royalist commander, Lord Crawford, decided to flee to Winchester, ostensibly to seek reinforcements. In his withdrawal Lord Crawford took the Royalist cavalry with him, and they were pursued for some distance by the Parliamentarian cavalry. Lord Crawford's withdrawal left Colonel Boles to mount a defence of Alton with just the Royalist infantry at his disposal.

Outnumbered and under artillery fire, the Royalist infantry were harried from one defensive position to the next, until they were finally corralled inside the church of St Lawrence, which would become the location of their last stand. Using horse carcasses as cover and also firing from the church windows, the Royalists mounted a defence of the church, whilst the Parliamentarians fired back and lobbed hand grenades through the church windows. The Royalist defence of the church was short lived and the Parliamentarians soon forced their way in. The remaining Royalists only surrendered on the death of Colonel Boles, who according to legend fought fiercely from the church's wooden pulpit until he was finally overcome and killed.

The damage caused to the church during the battle is still evident today for those with a keen eye. Musket holes from the fighting can been seen in the church door, as well as in other locations inside the church.

Musket holes in the church door from the Battle of Alton in 1643

The pulpit where Colonel Boles met his end

4.7 The Monmouth Rebellion

Satnav: Monmouth Beach, Lyme Regis, Dorset DT7 3LE

When the popular King Charles II died in 1685, the Crown passed to his unpopular brother, James II. Many people would have preferred to see Charles's eldest son, the Duke of Monmouth, on the throne, but the latter was an illegitimate child and hence ineligible for the Crown. Nevertheless, Monmouth – who had been living in exile in the Netherlands – decided to try to seize it by force.

On 11 June 1685, Monmouth arrived in the small Dorset coastal town of Lyme Regis with an "invasion force" of just 82 men. The place where he landed is now called Monmouth Beach, a popular spot with both holidaymakers and fossil hunters.

Monmouth Beach

Monmouth recruited more followers in Lyme Regis, then proceeded north through Dorset, Devon and Somerset. Along the way he gathered more "troops" – mainly young farmworkers armed with sickles and pitchforks! As described in the following item, Monmouth's haphazard rebellion came to an abrupt end at the Battle of Sedgemoor. Following this defeat, twelve of the rebels who had been recruited in Lyme Regis were publicly executed on Monmouth Beach.

4.8 Sedgemoor Battlefield

Satnav: Near Westonzoyland, Somerset TA7 0HG (approx)

The previous item described how the Duke of Monmouth's rebellion began on a Dorset beach on 11 June 1685. Despite its haphazard nature, the rebellion went surprisingly well for the first couple of weeks. By the time Monmouth's army of volunteer rebels reached Somerset, it had grown in size from a few dozen to over six thousand. Their first major strategic target was Bristol – England's second largest city at that time.

Unfortunately, few of the rebels had any military training, and most of them were still armed with farm implements rather than real weapons. After their first few encounters with the King's troops, their numbers began to drop dramatically, through a mixture of casualties and desertions. By the start of July the remaining rebels were hemmed in near Bridgwater in Somerset.

The Royalist troops gathered in the village of Westonzoyland, about four miles east of Bridgwater. They were comparable in numbers to the rebels – a few thousand – but much better armed, with muskets, artillery and cavalry. Nevertheless, Monmouth chose to attack them. The result was the distinctly one-sided affair known as the Battle of Sedgemoor – the last battle ever fought on English soil.

The site of the Battle of Sedgemoor

Weird History

The rebels attempted a surprise attack after nightfall on 6 July. Even with the element of surprise, however, they stood little chance against the far superior forces ranged against them. Approximately 1300 of Monmouth's supporters died on the battlefield, against less than 200 of the King's troops. In the days that followed, the surviving rebels were rounded up and captured – including the Duke of Monmouth himself, who was found hiding in a ditch near Horton in Dorset (see the entry on the Horton Tower in Chapter 3: *Weird Constructions*). Monmouth was executed in London on 15 July 1685.

Today, the site of the Battle of Sedgemoor is marked by an information board on the northern edge of Westonzoyland, and a war memorial in a nearby field. The latter consists of a central obelisk *"in memory of all those who doing the right as they gave it fell in the Battle of Sedgemoor"*, surrounded by four inscribed staddle stones. One of these commemorates the Battle of Sedgemoor itself; the other three refer to the battles of Plassey (1757) and Quebec (1759), those of Trafalgar (1805) and Waterloo (1815), and the two World Wars.

The Battle of Sedgemoor Memorial

There is also a Battle of Sedgemoor Visitor Centre inside St Mary's church in Westonzoyland, containing a wealth of information about the Monmouth Rebellion as well as historical artifacts and a panoramic reconstruction of the battle.

4.9 A Relic of the Napoleonic Wars

Satnav: Great Wishford church, Wiltshire SP2 0PH

The village of Great Wishford in Wiltshire has a series of odd stones embedded in the churchyard wall. On closer inspection, the stones appear to be a record of bread prices since the era of the Napoleonic Wars.

The stones can be seen bottom right, near the roadsign

The bread prices listed on the stones start in 1800, and the stones read as follows:

- 1800 Bread 3s 4d per Gall
- 1801 Bread 3s 10d per Gall
- 1904 Bread 10d per Gall
- 1920 Bread 2s 8d per Gallon After The Great War
- 1946-48 Bread Rationed Subsidised Price 2s 1d per Gall
- 1963 Bread 5s 4d per Gall
- 1971 Bread 8s per Gall – Decimal Currency 40p
- 1984 Bread £1.80 per Gall
- 2000 Bread £3.72 per Gall

"Gall" stands for gallons. It seems a bit odd that bread was measured in gallons, but presumably this is the dry volume of the ingredients (i.e. the flour). In the prices themselves, "s" stands for shilling, which was a twentieth of a pound, and "d" for (old) penny, which was a twelfth of a shilling.

The history of the stones seems to be that during the Napoleonic Wars the French tried to blockade Britain by exerting control over continental ports and seizing goods bound for Britain. This attempted blockade of Britain prevented the easy import of wheat, and led to a large rise in the price of bread. In an attempt to try to ensure transparency in his pricing, it is said that the local baker put his prices in stone in the churchyard wall. This tradition of recording bread prices in stone has continued ever since.

The record of bread prices

4.10 Morwellham Quay

Satnav: Morwellham Quay, Devon PL19 8JL (admission charge)

Morwellham Quay, about four miles south-west of Tavistock in Devon, is probably the closest thing in England to one of the ghost towns of the American Gold Rush. In this case, however, the rush was not for gold but for copper. When the Great Consols Copper Mine was opened a few miles away in 1844, Morwhellham, located on the River Tamar, became a strategic port for the distribution of freshly mined copper. In its heyday in the late 19th century, 30,000 tonnes of ore passed through the port every year.

By 1903, however, all the copper in the mine had been extracted and the business closed down. At the same time, the expansion of the railways meant there was no longer any call for inland ports such as Morwellham. The whole place was abandoned, becoming a literal ghost town.

For decades Morwellham was allowed to fall into disrepair, before an attempt was made to restore it to its former glory. It is now open to the public as a kind of time capsule of the Victorian industrial age, complete with a ship of the period, a waterwheel, worker's cottages, limekilns and parts of an elevated railway.

Morwellham Quay

5 Weird Landscape

The landscape of Wessex has been made partly by nature and partly by human civilization... and both have added their own touches of weirdness. The ten sites in this chapter are arranged thematically – the Iron Age hillforts of Old Sarum, Danebury, Maiden Castle and Ham Hill, the chalk hill figures of Westbury, Alton Barnes, Cerne Abbas, Osmington and Broad Town, and finally the recently formed natural landscape of the Lyme Regis undercliff.

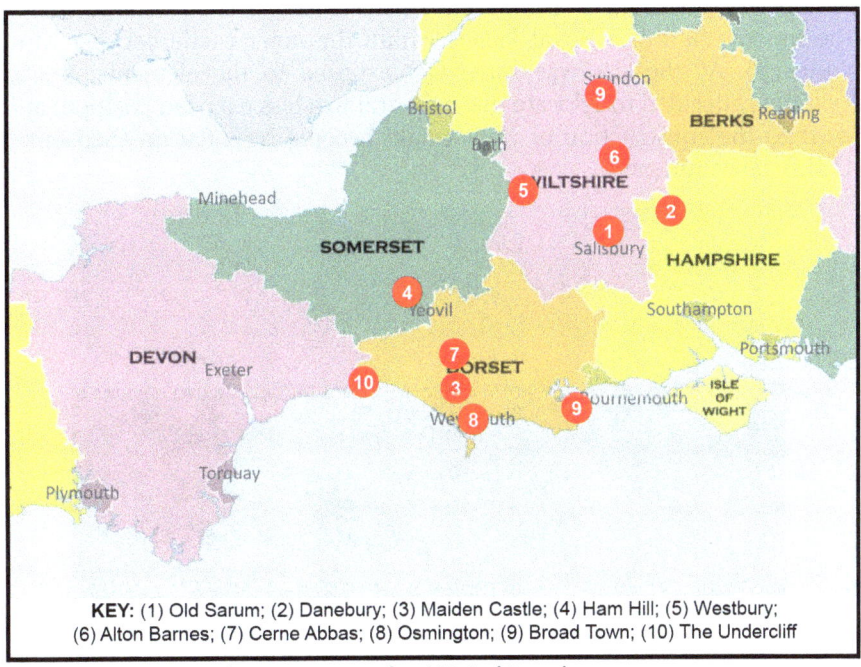

KEY: (1) Old Sarum; (2) Danebury; (3) Maiden Castle; (4) Ham Hill; (5) Westbury; (6) Alton Barnes; (7) Cerne Abbas; (8) Osmington; (9) Broad Town; (10) The Undercliff

Locator map for Weird Landscape

5.1 Old Sarum

Satnav: Old Sarum, Wiltshire SP1 3SD (English Heritage)

Old Sarum is an ancient site near Salisbury in Wiltshire. It started life as an Iron Age hill-fort, and following the Roman invasion of 43 AD it became the Roman settlement of Sorviodunum. Old Sarum remained in use as a fortified settlement during the Saxon era, and around 1069 the Normans erected a motte and baily castle on the site.

A cathedral was built at Old Sarum between 1075 and 1092, followed by the construction of a Royal Palace within the inner castle between 1130 and 1139. As the site was somewhat exposed to the elements, it was eventually decided to relocate the cathedral to a less exposed position, and in 1220 the construction of what would become New Sarum (Salisbury) Cathedral commenced.

The remains of the cathedral at Old Sarum

The general populace of Old Sarum followed the relocation of the cathedral, and Salisbury began to emerge as the preferred settlement. By 1240 the majority of the local population had abandoned Old Sarum in favour of Salisbury. Even though Old Sarum was now effectively population-less, it still retained the right to elect two members of parliament. As such Old Sarum became one of the most famous "Rotten Boroughs" in the land, with wealthy people owning land there to ensure they could become elected to parliament.

What many visitors to Old Sarum may miss is a stone monument on the opposite side of the A345, about half way between Old Sarum and the Portway roundabout. The monument is marked on Ordnance Survey maps with the cryptic label "Gun End of Base". The monument itself, however, clearly explains its purpose with the following inscription:

> *In 1794 a line from this site to Beacon Hill was measured by Capt W Mudge of the Ordnance Survey as a base for the triangulation of Great Britain.*

It seems that in 1794 Captain William Mudge (1762 – 1820), of the Royal Artillery, measured the distance between the site of the monument and nearby Beacon Hill, approximately 7 miles north east of Old Sarum. This measurement apparently became the baseline from which the first definitive mapping survey of Great Britain began.

The label "Gun End of Base" on Ordnance Survey maps apparently refers to the spot at which a cannon was buried vertically in the ground. It seems that Captain Mudge would have used the buried cannon to erect his theodolite on, prior to him making his measurements.

The Ordnance Survey monument

5.2 Danebury Hill-Fort

Satnav: Danebury Hill-Fort, near Stockbridge, Hampshire SO20 8HQ (approx)

One thing the Wessex landscape offers in abundance is Iron Age hill-forts. One of the most famous of these can be found at Danebury in Hampshire, near the village of Nether Wallop and about ten miles south of Andover.

Danebury hill-fort covers an area of about 12 acres, and is believed to have been built in the 6th century BC and to have been in use for about 500 years. At its height Danebury would have been home to a community of 300 to 400 people. Archaeological excavations between 1969 and 1988 uncovered extensive evidence of occupation, including over 180,000 pieces of pottery and 240,000 pieces of animal bone. Like most hill-forts, Danebury was abandoned around 100 BC. The reason for the general abandonment of hill-forts in this era is still a matter of debate.

The entrance to Danebury hill-fort

5.3 Maiden Castle

Satnav: Maiden Castle Road, Dorchester, Dorset DT1 2HH (approx)
(English Heritage)

A sign at the entrance to Maiden Castle, just outside Dorchester, claims that it is the largest and most complex hill-fort in Britain. It encloses an area the size of 50 football fields, and was home to several hundred people during the Iron Age between 800 BC and the coming of the Romans in 43 AD.

Initially there was nothing especially remarkable about Maiden Castle, which started out on a similar scale to other hill-forts in the area. But around 550 BC it was massively expanded in size, and the defences were built up into multiple ramparts and ditches. These are believed to have been added more by way of a status symbol than for any military reason!

The multiple ramparts of Maiden Castle

The hill-fort was abandoned after the Roman invasion in the 1st century AD. Then in the 4th century, towards the end of the Roman occupation, a temple complex was built on top of the hill. By this time, the local religion had evolved into a fusion of Roman and native British beliefs. This resulted in the construction of new temples such as the one at Maiden Castle, and the smaller temple at Jordan Hill near Weymouth.

The Maiden Castle temple consisted of a central room, roughly square in plan, surrounded by an outer corridor called an ambulatory. There was also a separate two-room building, which was probably the priest's house, and an oval hut which may have contained a shrine.

Numerous archaeological finds have been made in and around the temple, including hoards of coins and statues. Many of these may have been offerings to the deity to whom the temple was dedicated – possibly the goddess Minerva, as was the case in Roman Bath (see Chapter 1: *Weird Archaeology*).

The remains of the Roman Temple

5.4 Ham Hill

Satnav: Ham Hill Country Park, Somerset TA14 6RW

Just west of Yeovil in Somerset is Ham Hill, a large Iron Age hill-fort that boasts one of the newest sets of standing stones in England.

The hill-fort is an impressive construction with a double bank and ditch design; it has three miles of ramparts rising in places to 12 metres in height. The ramparts defend an approximate area of 210 acres and the hill-fort sits at around 120 m above sea level, with commanding views of the surrounding landscape.

Archaeological evidence points to the hill-fort having been built initially in the 7th Century BC, and subsequently occupied during the Roman era. It may have fallen into disuse during the Saxon period, but it was used again in late mediaeval times, after the Norman conquest.

Today, another notable feature at Ham Hill is the circle of standing stones, made from locally quarried ham stone. These stones are a modern creation, having been erected in 2000 to commemorate the workers who have quarried stone at Ham Hill over the centuries.

The Stone Circle at Ham Hill

5.5 Westbury White Horse

Satnav: Near Bratton, Wiltshire BA13 4TA (approx)

The Westbury White Horse is thought to be the second oldest in England, after the prehistoric chalk figure at Uffington (see Chapter 1: *Weird Archaeology*). It can be found a mile and a half east of the town of Westbury in Wiltshire, just below the Iron Age hill-fort known as Bratton Camp.

Legend suggests that the white horse was originally carved to commemorate King Alfred's victory at the Battle of Edington in 878 (see the entry on Stourhead in Chapter 3: *Weird Constructions*). Alfred was supposedly born near the Uffington White Horse, and this may have provided inspiration for the Westbury horse – although there is no firm evidence for the existence of a chalk figure at Westbury before the year 1742.

The Westbury White Horse

Westbury's horse seems to have evolved over time. An engraving from the 1760s depicts the figure of a horse at the site, but it is smaller than today and facing in the opposite direction. Over the years the horse has been slowly remodelled and "improved", with the original chalk carving slowly morphing into the low-maintenance concreted-over horse that can be seen today.

5.6 Alton Barnes

Satnav: Alton Barnes, Wiltshire SN8 4LB (approx)

The landscape around Alton Barnes in Wiltshire is best known today as the epicentre of British crop circle activity (see the entry for the Barge Inn in Chapter 8: *Weird Science*). However, it also has a more venerable landscape feature in the form of a giant white horse, which was cut into the chalk in 1812. The horse can be found about a mile north of the village of Alton Barnes, etched into the side of Milk Hill – the highest point in Wiltshire, almost 1000 feet above sea level. From the summit of Milk Hill another nearby white horse, at Pewsey, can also be seen – that one dates from 1937.

Alton Barnes White Horse

A much older landscape feature can be found about 500 metres south east of the white horse. This is a Neolithic long barrow known as Adam's Grave. Over the years it has been badly damaged by farming, so is not as impressive to view as the long barrows at West Kennet and Wayland's Smithy (see Chapter 1: *Weird Archaeology*). However, its outline is still clearly visible in aerial photographs.

In Saxon times, Adam's Grave was known as Wodensburg. According to the Anglo-Saxon chronicle, King Ceawlin of Wessex was defeated in battle there in 592 AD. More recently, the fields around Adam's Grave have become popular sites for crop circle activity!

Adam's Grave

5.7 The Cerne Giant

Satnav: Cerne Abbas, Dorset DT2 7AL (National Trust)

The Cerne Giant is one of the best known features of the Dorset landscape. In fact it's such a familiar image that it's easy to forget just how bizarre and unique it is. The artistic depiction of a sexually aroused male, while not unknown in other parts of the world, is extremely rare in Britain. Chalk hill figures depicting human figures, as opposed to horses, are also very rare – the only other example comparable to the Cerne Giant is the Long Man of Wilmington in East Sussex. And the Long Man of Wilmington doesn't have his genitalia on display.

The Cerne Giant

Perhaps the most contentious question about the Cerne Giant is its age. Of Britain's chalk figures, only the Uffington White Horse (see Chapter 1: *Weird Archaeology*) has been accurately dated to prehistoric times. Most of the others are a few centuries old at most. As regards the Cerne Giant, the earliest record of it dates from the second half of the 17th century. One theory is that it's a political caricature dating from around that time. But the style of the image simply doesn't look like it comes from the 17th century – a puritanical period in English history when artistic nudity of any kind was frowned upon.

A more credible suggestion is that the Giant is much older – either Roman or pre-Roman – and that over the centuries it became overgrown and lost to view until it was rediscovered in the 17th century. The village of Cerne Abbas was attached to a mediaeval abbey, and it's difficult to believe the monks would have done any proactive maintenance work on the Giant – they may even have deliberately tried to obliterate it.

There are similarities between the Giant and traditional depictions of Hercules. The ancient Greek hero, who was also popular with the Romans, was often depicted holding a club in one hand and a lion skin in the other. Archaeological evidence does indeed suggest that the Cerne Giant might once have held a lion skin (or something similar) which has since been erased. However, Hercules isn't usually depicted with an enormous erection. So it may be that the Cerne Giant originated in pre-Roman times – perhaps around the same time as the Uffington White Horse – and was later adapted by the Romans into a depiction of Hercules.

5.8 Osmington White Horse

Satnav: Osmington Hill, Weymouth, Dorset DT3 6ED

The White Horse on Osmington Hill just outside Weymouth is unusual among Britain's chalk hill figures for two reasons. Firstly the horse is shown with a rider, and secondly the identity of both horse and rider are known.

The Osmington White Horse

The hill figure was created in 1808 to commemorate the frequent visits to Weymouth of King George III, who liked to ride over the surrounding hills on his favourite horse, Adonis. It was only during George's reign that the idea of "seaside holidays" started to become popular, and his regular visits to Weymouth transformed it into one of the most fashionable seaside resorts in England. In gratitude for this, a group of locals decided to immortalise both George and Adonis in the traditional form of a hill figure. Unfortunately, by the time it was finished the king was chronically ill, so he was never able to come back to Weymouth to see his chalk counterpart.

In size, Osmington's White Horse is second only to the prehistoric white horse of Uffington (see Chapter 1: *Weird Archaeology*). It is 85 metres long and 98 metres high – almost as tall as St Paul's Cathedral in London.

The biggest threat to its existence came in 1989, when a misguided "makeover" staged by a TV show saw the chalk figure covered in 160 tonnes of limestone chippings. The immediate effect of this was indeed to enhance the figure's appearance, but over time the chippings began to slide down the hill causing severe damage to the original outline.

By 2009 the horse was in such poor condition that a group of local volunteers began to restore it properly, removing the limestone chippings and bringing out the original chalk carving. This work was completed in March 2012, a few months before Weymouth was due to host the Olympic sailing events. The following year, a special viewing area was opened on the A353 between Osmington and Weymouth.

The white horse seen from Weymouth beach

5.9 Broad Town White Horse

Satnav: Broad Town, Wiltshire SN4 7RD (approx)

With the proliferation of chalk figures in the English countryside, it is easy to forget that they would soon become obscured from sight if they were not carefully maintained. One of the authors (Paul Jackson) had first-hand experience of this in June 2014 when the white horse at Broad Town in Wiltshire was refurbished by local volunteers.

The Broad Town White Horse is situated on a hillside about half a mile northeast of Broad Town, and is believed to date from 1864 (there is another similar figure, possibly slightly older, called the Hackpen White Horse at Broad Hinton a few miles away).

There are two reasons why the Broad Town White Horse requires constant maintenance. Firstly, because the field is not grazed by livestock, the outline of the horse is constantly under threat of becoming overgrown. This unrelenting march of nature means that twice a year the chalk figure has to be weeded and trimmed to ensure it retains its shape and crisp outline, otherwise after a few short years it would be lost from view. Secondly, the horse would have appeared a brilliant white when it was originally cut into the chalk, but over time the colour tends to yellow. Hence it has to be re-limed on an annual basis to ensure it retains its former glory.

The white horse after restoration

5.10 The Undercliff

Satnav: Footpath from Holmbush car park, Lyme Regis, Dorset DT7 3JL

Up to this point, the *Weird Landscape* chapter has focused on instances where the natural landscape has been reshaped by human hands, whether by the construction of hill-forts or gigantic chalk figures. To finish off, here is an example of the exact opposite – where nature has transformed a human-tamed landscape of neatly cultivated fields and gardens into a veritable jungle.

The Undercliff "jungle"

The cliffs between Lyme Regis and Axmouth always had a tendency to erosion and subsidence, but that didn't stop local farmers making best use of the land at the top of the cliffs. By the early 19th century the area was packed with market gardens, orchards, sheep and pig farms and hazel coppices. Then in the space of a few hours on Christmas Day, 1839, the whole thing came crashing down in one of the biggest landslides in recorded history. An estimated 8 million tonnes of rock and earth collapsed into the sea, along a stretch of coast about four miles long.

It's fortunate that the landslip occurred during the biggest holiday of the year, because it meant no-one was working in the fields so there were very few casualties. But all that carefully cultivated farmland was lost forever. In its place was a rocky, barren landscape the like of which had never been seen before. Within weeks, people were travelling from miles away to view the scene. The local farmers, sensing a way to cut their losses, quickly took to charging visitors sixpence a time to enter their fields!

The ultimate cause of the landslip was underground water loosening the clay on which the upper rock strata sat. Some geologists at the time realised this, but many ordinary people believed it was an earthquake – possibly even a sign of God's wrath!

The area of the landslip, which became known as the Undercliff, was too treacherously unstable for human cultivation. Since the middle of the 19th century it has been left completely in the hands of nature, resulting in the closest thing to a jungle that it's possible to find in modern-day England.

Since 1955 the 800 acre site has been a National Nature Reserve. It is only accessible from two points, about five miles apart – one at the western end near Axmouth and the other at the eastern end near Lyme Regis. The two points are joined by a long, winding footpath which is quite often closed at some point due to further subsidence. All but the most determined explorers would do best to enter at the Lyme Regis end, walk as far as they want to go, and then turn round and return to their starting point.

The path through the Undercliff

6 Weird Legends

Some of the legends of Wessex are well known, such as those telling of the exploits of King Arthur and his knights. Others are much less familiar, and may even come as a surprise to many locals. The ten entries in this chapter are arranged chronologically: the ancient Trojan legends of Totnes and Plymouth, the Arthurian legends of Glastonbury, Cadbury Castle and Winchester, the mediaeval legends of Athelney and Shebbear, and finally the latter-day legends of Tedworth House, Alton and Brockenhurst.

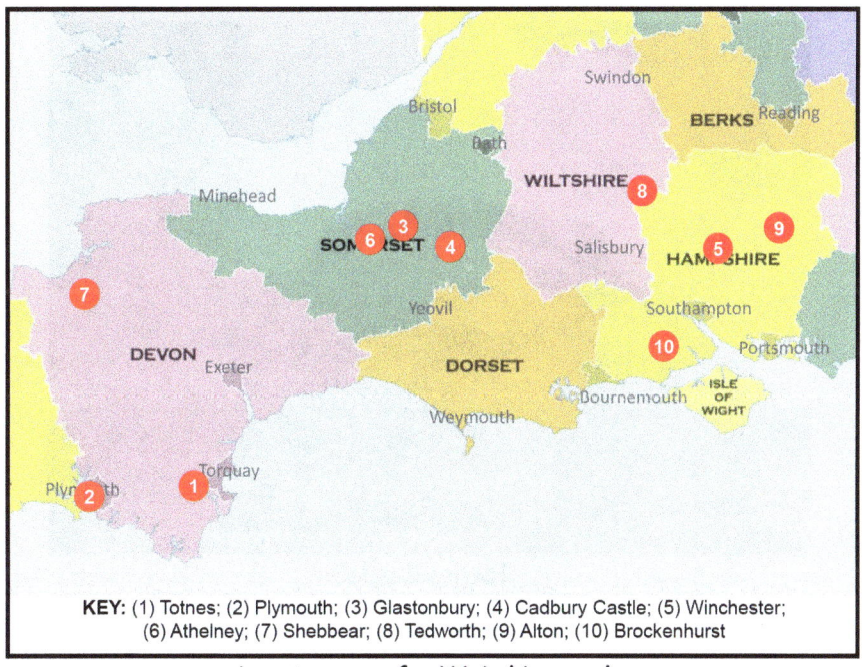

KEY: (1) Totnes; (2) Plymouth; (3) Glastonbury; (4) Cadbury Castle; (5) Winchester; (6) Athelney; (7) Shebbear; (8) Tedworth; (9) Alton; (10) Brockenhurst

Locator map for Weird Legends

6.1 The Brutus Stone

Satnav: Totnes town centre, Devon TQ9 5NL

Totnes is a small market town about eight miles from the mouth of the River Dart on the south coast of Devon. These days it is best known as a centre of alternative culture, with an abundance of "New Age" teachers and natural health practitioners. However, the town has a long history, stretching back at least to 907 AD when Totnes Castle was constructed. According to local legend, however, the site is much older than that.

Totnes Castle

The legendary founder of Britain, from whom the name of the country is derived, was Brutus of Troy, supposedly one of the grandsons of the great Trojan hero Aeneas. The Trojans were immortalized in the epics of ancient Greece and Rome, and Aeneas himself is said to have fought against the Greeks in the Trojan War more than ten millennia ago. Just as Aeneas was the legendary founder of Rome, so his grandson is said to have founded Britain.

The earliest known mention of the Brutus legend can be found in a book by Nennius called *Historia Brittonum*, dating from the 9th century AD. A more detailed version of the story was provided by Geoffrey of Monmouth in his *History of the Kings of Britain*, which was written around 1136.

According to Geoffrey's account, Brutus first stepped ashore at Totnes. Later retellings added even more details to the legend, such as the first words spoken by Brutus in the newly discovered country: *"Here I stand and here I rest. And this town shall be called Totnes."*

The point at which Brutus first stepped ashore is marked to this day by a small granite boulder called the "Brutus Stone", set into the pavement of Fore Street. This is a long way from the river today, but may have been closer to it in the past. The association of the stone with Brutus was first mentioned in 1697, long after Nennius and Geoffrey first recorded the legend.

The Brutus Stone

6.2 Plymouth Hoe

Satnav: Plymouth Hoe, Devon PL1 2JG

Totnes is not the only place in Devon associated with ancient Troy. Another legendary connection with the Trojans can be found in the city of Plymouth on Devon's south coast.

According to Geoffrey of Monmouth, when Brutus and his fellow Trojans landed at Totnes, they were the first humans to set foot in the British Isles. But that's not to say Britain was completely uninhabited at the time – the locals consisted of a race of ferocious giants. According to legend, a major battle took place between the giants and the newly arrived Trojans in the area now known as Plymouth Hoe. This is familiar to all British schoolchildren as the place where Sir Francis Drake finished his game of bowls before sailing off to defeat the Spanish Armada in 1588.

Statue of Drake on Plymouth Hoe

The leader of the Trojan forces was a man named Corineus, while the locals were led by a particularly large giant named Gogmagot. The latter name is sometimes spelled Gogmagog, through confusion with the Biblical giants Gog and Magog. However, Gogmagot had nothing to do with the Bible – the name is probably derived from the Celtic *Gawr Madoc*, or Madoc the Great. As the legend goes, after a long and heated battle the Trojans finally managed to defeat the giants. In a feat of superhuman strength, Corineus hurled Gogmagot to his death on the rocks below.

The story of Gogmagot and Corineus is just a legend, of course. But it's a matter of historic fact that for hundreds of years there was at least one, and possibly two, giant figures carved into the rock of Plymouth Hoe. The larger figure, representing Gogmagot, was first recorded in 1496, and was described as being "12 cubits" in size: the exact dimensions given by Geoffrey of Monmouth for Gogmagot (a mediaeval cubit was half a yard, or 18 inches). The figure would still have been visible at the time of the Spanish Armada in 1588, and when the Mayflower set sail for the New World in 1620. However, they were obliterated in the 1660s when the Royal Citadel was constructed on the Hoe – a huge stone fortress which is still standing today.

Plymouth Hoe (the Royal Citadel is behind the lighthouse)

6.3 Glastonbury Tor

Satnav: Glastonbury, Somerset BA6 8BG

Glastonbury Tor is a hill that stands prominently in the flat landscape of the Somerset levels. Archaeological evidence suggests that it has been regularly visited since prehistory, and a number of buildings are believed to have been constructed on the summit during the Saxon period. At one time a timber church, dedicated to St Michael, was present on the summit of the Tor, but it was destroyed during an earthquake in 1275. A sandstone church (also dedicated to St Michael) was built on the Tor in 1323, surviving until the dissolution of the monasteries in 1539. During this turbulent period the last Abbot of Glastonbury, Richard Whiting, was hung, drawn and quartered – possibly on the Tor itself – along with two other monks. Today, only the three-story roofless tower of the sandstone church remains standing on the exposed summit of the hill.

Glastonbury Tor

Aside from its known history, Glastonbury Tor is also associated with a number of legends. Foremost among these is the suggestion that the Tor is the mythical Isle of Avalon from Arthurian legend. As mentioned in the entry for Glastonbury Abbey in Chapter 1: *Weird Archaeology*, an inscription was discovered in 1191 that read: *"Here lieth buried the famous King Arthur in the Isle of Avalon"*. As the Tor resides on the Somerset levels flood plain, it is possible that it may, at one time, have been surrounded by water, literally making it an island.

The ruins of St Michael's church

The Tor has also been claimed as the last resting place of the Holy Grail, which was supposedly brought to Britain by Joseph of Arimathea after the crucifixion of Jesus. Some stories even suggest that Jesus himself may have visited Glastonbury in his youth!

The Holy Grail is supposed to be the cup, or chalice, that was used to collect some of Christ's blood following the crucifixion. This legend is echoed in the name of Chalice Well, which can be found a short distance from Glastonbury Tor. The waters from this well are rich in iron oxide, which gives it a distinctly reddish hue – which was interpreted in the Middle Ages as Holy Blood, and evidence that the Grail was nearby!

6.4 Cadbury Castle

Satnav: South Cadbury, Somerset BA22 7HA

The hill-fort of Cadbury Castle lies in the Somerset village of South Cadbury. It was built during the Iron Age, around 500 BC, and was continuously occupied until it was overrun by the Romans in the 1st century AD, in what seems to have been a particularly brutal and violent event. According to the Somerset County Council website, there is "clear evidence of destruction by fire and the massacre of a group of inhabitants". However, after the departure of the Romans, the South Cadbury site was reoccupied and redeveloped in the early Middle Ages.

Cadbury Castle

In 1533, a man named John Leland was given a commission by King Henry VIII "to make a search after England's Antiquities". This assignment took him to all corners of the country, including South Cadbury, where he wrote *"At the very south end of the church of South Cadbury standeth Camelot, sometime a famous town or castle"* and that *"The people can tell nothing there but that they have heard say that Arthur much restored to Camelot."*

In other words, Leland was saying that Cadbury Castle was nothing less than King Arthur's Camelot! Whether this is true or not is a matter of debate. There is no historical consensus as to what century Arthur lived in, what kingdom he ruled over, or even if he existed in the real world at all. One opinion holds that he was King of Dumnonia – roughly corresponding to modern-day Cornwall, Devon and Somerset – around 500 AD. According to this view, it's not unreasonable to suggest that Cadbury Castle might have been associated with King Arthur – possibly even one of his main courts.

Cadbury Castle lies close to what would have been the heavily defended border of Dumnonia and Wessex. The name Cadbury means "Cado's Fort", Cado being a king of Dumnonia who was in power around the time Arthur was born. Archaeological evidence indicates that the site was massively refortified during this period, with a palatial timber-framed Great Hall erected at its centre – the court of Camelot, maybe?

These days, the only structure on top of Cadbury Castle is a stone plinth dated "2000 AD". The plaque on top of this shows the directions and distances to a number of other places of interest, several of which feature in this book. There are the megalithic sites of Stonehenge and Avebury (Chapter 1: *Weird Archaeology*), the hill-forts of Ham Hill and Maiden Castle (Chapter 5: *Weird Landscape*) and Alfred's Tower near Stourhead (Chapter 3: *Weird Constructions*), as well as Glastonbury which featured in the preceding item.

The Cadbury Castle plinth

6.5 Winchester's Round Table

Satnav: Winchester Great Hall, Hampshire SO23 8UJ

The "Great Hall" in Winchester is all that remains today of Winchester Castle. Originally built in 1067 for William the Conqueror, the castle was improved over the years, with the Great Hall that stands today being built in the early 13th century to replace the original hall.

The castle's downfall occurred in 1646 during the English Civil War, when Parliamentarians captured the castle from Royalist forces. Following this victory Oliver Cromwell had the castle demolished. The Great Hall was given a stay of execution and the building was preserved as a venue for assemblies and the County Assizes.

Winchester Great Hall

Over its lifetime the Great Hall has been the venue of some important events. In 1603 Sir Walter Raleigh stood trial at the Great Hall for his suspected part in a plot to remove King James I from the throne. More recently Lord Montagu of Beaulieu, Major Michael Pitt-Rivers and Peter Wildeblood were tried and convicted in 1954 on charges of "conspiracy to incite certain male persons to commit serious offences with male persons"!

The most striking feature of the Great Hall is the Arthurian Round Table which hangs at one end of the hall. The table is believed to have been constructed around 1250 to 1290, during the reign of Edward I. The current paintwork on the table was commissioned by Henry VIII for the visit of the Holy Roman Emperor Charles V in 1522. The artwork shows the names of 24 knights of King Arthur's court, with Henry VIII himself sitting in King Arthur's seat at the 12 o'clock position. At 18 feet in diameter, the round table would have been an imposing piece of furniture.

The Winchester Round Table

Arthurian legend was popular across Europe during the Middle Ages, and jousting festivals called "Round Tables" were often held. Presumably it was for such events that replica round tables were made. Edward I was an Arthurian enthusiast himself, who attended a number of Round Tables and even hosted one himself in 1299. It is possible the Winchester Round Table was created for this event, although there is also evidence it was made for a tournament in 1290 to mark the betrothal of one of the king's daughters.

Although the Winchester Round Table is clearly not the original table used at King Arthur's court, if it ever existed, it is certainly one of the earliest surviving replicas still in existence.

6.6 King Alfred's Monument

Satnav: Athelney, Somerset TA7 0SD (approx)

The village of Athelney in Somerset lies on slightly higher ground than its surroundings. The name means "island of the princes", and it would indeed have been a kind of island in the days when the Somerset Levels were regularly flooded. Athelney was fortified with bank and ditch defences during the Iron Age, making it the lowest hill-fort in England!

Athelney's strongest historical association is with King Alfred the Great. Early in 878 AD, most of Alfred's Wessex kingdom was overrun by the marauding Viking army of Guthrum. Alfred was pushed back into the Somerset Levels, where he established a stronghold at Athelney. According to legend, when Alfred first arrived in Somerset he was taken in by a local peasant woman. When she left him on his own to watch some baking cakes, Alfred's mind drifted onto more strategic matters and he allowed the cakes to burn. This may be the only "fact" many people know about King Alfred!

Today, all that can be seen above ground at Athelney is a monument erected in 1801, which is best viewed from a layby on the A361 a short distance to the north.

King Alfred's Monument

Weird Legends

Alfred used his time at Athelney to plan a counter-attack against Guthrum's army, which he successfully carried out at the Battle of Edington a few months later (see the entry on Stourhead and King Alfred's Tower in Chapter 3: *Weird Constructions*). This allowed him to re-establish control over the entire kingdom of Wessex, centred around the city of Winchester in Hampshire. A thousand years after Alfred's death in 899, a suitably imposing statue of him was erected in the centre of that city.

Statue of Alfred the Great in Winchester

6.7 The Devil's Stone

Satnav: Shebbear, Devon EX21 5RU

Shebbear is a village in North Devon with an unusual piece of local folklore. On a patch of grass just outside the churchyard lies a large boulder, estimated to weigh about a tonne. The stone is believed to be a glacial erratic – a rock that was transported to the area by prehistoric glacial movements.

According to local folklore, however, the stone arrived in the village as a result of a battle between the Devil and God – a battle the Devil lost. It seems the Devil dropped the stone during the conflict, and it fell on top of him and flattened him under it.

The local tradition states that it takes a year for the Devil to dig down and then back up the other side of the stone, and so every year the village bell ringers flip the stone over in a bid to re-trap the Devil and protect the village from harm. This stone flipping ceremony occurs on the 5th November every year, in an alternative celebration to the typical Guy Fawkes night antics of bonfires and fireworks.

The Devil's Stone of Shebbear

6.8 The Tedworth Drummer

Satnav: Tidworth, Wiltshire SP9 7AJ (house not open to public)

Tedworth House is located in the small town of Tidworth, previously known as Tedworth, which lies on the Wiltshire/Hampshire border. Its main claim to fame is that it was the scene of one of the earliest recorded examples of poltergeist activity, back in the 17th century.

At the time of the events in question, the house was owned by a man named Mompesson. In 1662, four years after the death of Oliver Cromwell and two years after the restoration of Charles II, Mompesson had a dispute with a vagrant who had been a drummer in Cromwell's army. The upshot of the dispute was that the drummer was sent to prison – but that wasn't the end of the affair.

While the drummer was supposed to be safely incarcerated, Mompesson's house became the target of a barrage of unexplained phenomena from drummings and other noises to sulphurous smells, strange lights and objects being hurled around. These phenomena were blamed on the drummer, who was said to have used witchcraft to summon an evil spirit, or demon – the case has gone down in legend as "the Demon Drummer of Tedworth".

The Tedworth case was investigated by a pioneer of "paranormal research" named Joseph Glanvill. It features prominently in his book *Saducismus Triumphatus: Full and Plain Evidence Concerning Witches and Apparitions*, which was published posthumously in 1681.

Tedworth House

6.9 Sweet Fanny Adams

Satnav: Alton cemetery, Hampshire GU34 2EB

The town cemetery of Alton in Hampshire contains a gravestone commemorating a brutal murder that gave rise to a famous 19th century urban legend. The inscription on the gravestone reads:

> *Sacred to the memory of Fanny Adams aged 8 years and 4 months who was cruelly murdered on Saturday August 24th 1867.*
>
> *"Fear not them which kill the body but are not able to kill the soul but rather fear Him which is able to destroy both body and soul in hell." Matthew 10 v 28.*

It seems that on Saturday 24 August 1867, the eight-year-old Fanny Adams was out walking along Tanhouse Lane in Alton with her friend, also aged 8, and her sister aged 7. During the course of this walk they encountered a local solicitor's clerk named Frederick Baker. After offering the girls some money, Baker abducted Fanny and took her into a nearby field.

When the other two girls returned home without Fanny the alarm was raised and Fanny's mother and a neighbour went up the lane to find her. Walking up the lane they encountered Baker but did not suspect him of any wrongdoing due to his respectability in the community.

The search for Fanny continued into the early evening and her body was eventually found in the field. It is said that her body had been butchered, with her head, legs and eyes removed and her torso emptied of its organs. Over the course of the next few days all of her missing body parts where eventually found.

Baker was duly arrested, and although he claimed innocence, he apparently had blood on his shirt and trousers and was in possession of two blood-stained knives. The piece of evidence that finally removed doubt of his guilt was his diary entry for the day, which read *"24th August, Saturday – killed a young girl. It was fine and hot."* At his trial Baker was found guilty of the murder and he was hung on 24th December 1867 outside Winchester Jail.

The horrible nature of this murder, and the widespread reporting of the crime, led to the birth of a bizarre urban legend. In 1869 new rations of tinned mutton were introduced into the British Navy, and they were widely reviled by the sailors. It was rumoured that some parts of Fanny's body had found their way into this new tinned provision! As a result, the phrase "Sweet Fanny Adams" sprang up as a slang term for this worthless form of tinned meat. Over the years this phrase, often shortened to "Sweet FA", came to mean "nothing at all".

If you want to find the grave of Sweet FA for yourself, then Alton cemetery can be found on Old Odiham Road. Fanny's gravestone is in the south side of the cemetery, to the north of Spitalfields Road.

The grave of Sweet Fanny Adams

6.10 The Snake Catcher's Grave

Satnav: Church Lane, Brockenhurst, Hampshire SO42 7UD

St Nicholas' churchyard in Brockenhurst, Hampshire, is home to an unusual white marble headstone, depicting an old bearded man in a wide-brimmed hat holding a handful of snakes, standing outside what appears to be a crude hut in a forest.

Harry Mills was born in 1840, and for the early part of his life he lived in the village of Emery Down, where he worked as a labourer. In his forties, however, he moved into an old charcoal burner's hut in the New Forest, just to the north of Brockenhurst, and embarked on a new occupation as a snake catcher. Armed only with a sack and a forked stick, Mills offered his services to rid the grounds of local properties of snakes! Word gradually spread about Mills and his eccentric ways, and he became something of a living legend. It was said that during his 18-year snake catching career he caught an astounding 30,000 grass snakes and 4,000 adders – many of them being sold on to London Zoo as fodder for their animals.

The Snake Catcher's gravestone

7 Weird Religion

This chapter contains a miscellany of unusual sights to be found in and around churches in the Wessex region. The ten entries are grouped thematically: the mediaeval oddities of Knowlton, Whitchurch Canonicorum, Stoke-sub-Hamdon and Langton Cross, the bizarre church decorations of Muchelney, Bishops Cannings and Crewkerne, and finally the weird memorials of Nether Wallop, Portesham and Abbotts Ann.

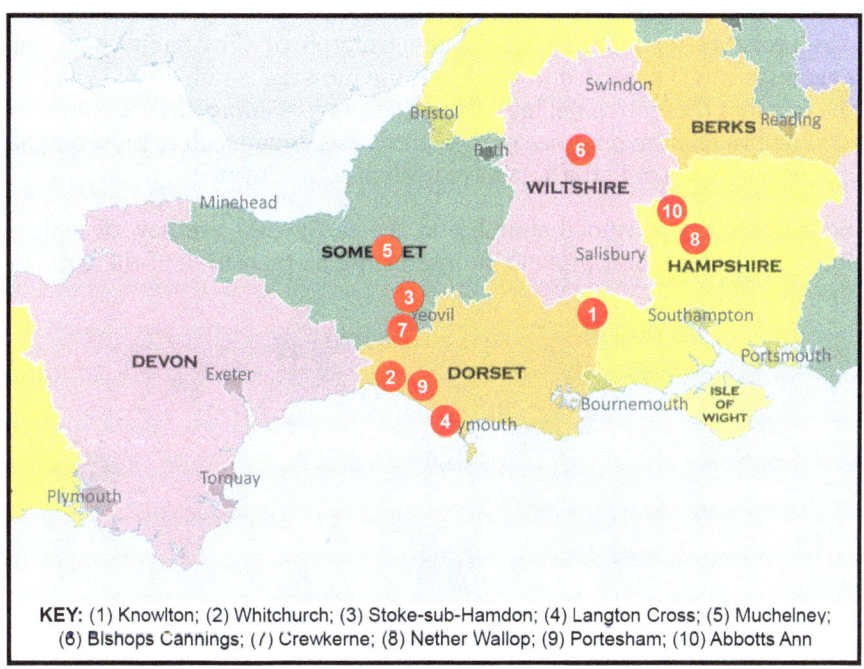

KEY: (1) Knowlton; (2) Whitchurch; (3) Stoke-sub-Hamdon; (4) Langton Cross; (5) Muchelney; (6) Bishops Cannings; (7) Crewkerne; (8) Nether Wallop; (9) Portesham; (10) Abbotts Ann

Locator map for Weird Religion

7.1 Knowlton Church and Earthworks

Satnav: Knowlton, Dorset BH21 5AE (English Heritage)

The parish church at Knowlton in Dorset dates from the Norman period, almost a thousand years ago. However, it was built on top of an even older religious site – a Neolithic henge constructed around four thousand years earlier!

The idea of building a church on a prehistoric site is highly unusual, and was probably intended to signify the triumph of Christianity over the Paganism which preceded it. However, the message is rather weakened by the fact that the church fell into disuse in the 17th century, and now stands in ruins! In fact the presence of the church has done much to preserve the henge, while others in the area have been ploughed over.

Both the folly-like ruined church and the earthworks are now owned by English Heritage, and provide an interesting juxtaposition of the old and the even older!

Knowlton church and henge

7.2 Whitchurch Canonicorum

Satnav: Whitchurch Canonicorum, Dorset DT6 6RQ

Whitchurch Canonicorum is a small village a few miles west of Bridport in Dorset. It was founded in Saxon times by Alfred the Great, who called it *Hwitan Cyrican*, meaning "white church". Nothing remains of the original Saxon church, but the present building, dating from the 12th to 15th century, has more than its fair share of weirdness – including the relics of a saint!

There are only two places in the country known to contain the mortal remains of a saint. One is Westminster Abbey in London; the other is the church of St Candida and Holy Cross in Whitchurch Canonicorum. Candida is the Latin word for "white", and the saint herself is more often referred to as "St Wite". The only inscription visible on her shrine is a modern one: *Hic reqesct reliqe Sce Wite* ("Here rest the relics of St Wite") – apparently duplicating the Latin inscription on a lead casket found inside the tomb when it was opened in 1900.

The shrine of St Wite

The tomb itself is very plain, which may be why it escaped destruction during the Reformation, when so many other shrines around the country were destroyed. Its only distinguishing feature is the presence of three oval-shaped orifices, where people can place prayer cards and other offerings to the saint. Virtually nothing is known about St Wite herself, but local legend has it that she was a Saxon wise-woman who was murdered by the Vikings.

Close-up of the shrine

The main part of the present church dates from the 12th and 13th centuries, when the legend of the Holy Grail was at the height of its popularity (see the entry on Glastonbury in Chapter 6: *Weird Legends*). But despite its Christian theme, the legend was rarely depicted in church art of the time. Nevertheless, there is a carving of a two-handled vessel on the outside wall of the church which is traditionally identified as the Grail.

The Holy Grail

Moving to more recent times, the churchyard contains one gravestone with a bilingual inscription – English on one side, Cyrillic on the other. This is the last resting place of Georgi Markov, a Bulgarian journalist who was murdered in London in 1978. He was waiting at a bus stop on his way to the BBC World Service, where he worked at the time, when he felt a stinging sensation in the back of his leg. He turned round to see a man pointing an umbrella at him. It turned out the umbrella concealed an air gun which had fired a pellet of the deadly poison Ricin into his leg; four days later Markov died in hospital.

The two sides of Markov's grave

7.3 A Mediaeval Dragon-Slayer

Satnav: Stoke-sub-Hamdon church, Somerset TA14 6UF

The village of Stoke-sub-Hamdon is located about five miles west of Yeovil in Somerset. It gets its odd-sounding name from the fact that it lies "under" Ham Hill, which featured in Chapter 5: *Weird Landscape*. The village church of Stoke-sub-Hamdon is dedicated to St Mary the Virgin, and the oldest parts of it date from Norman times, around the year 1100.

Probably dating from this period is a carving on the outside of the church, depicting a man battling a dragon. This is a curious motif to find on a Christian church, and is particularly striking for the way the arched back of the dragon fits neatly over the arch of the window – which is unusually narrow, even for the Norman period. Also noteworthy is the cartoony style of the image, which is reminiscent of the Bayeux tapestry from around the same time.

The Dragon carving

The carving is on the north side of the church, which was considered the "dark side" in mediaeval times, where Pagan imagery was often tucked away. Although dragons were common in Pagan folklore, this particular image may represent a Christianized legend. Some authors identify it as "St Michael and the dragon" and others as "St George and the dragon". But St George is normally depicted on horseback, so the first is more likely (a hill about a mile from the church is called St Michael's Hill, which adds further support to this idea). The story of St Michael and the dragon comes from the Book of Revelation; the dragon is Satan himself, whom St Michael consigns to Hell.

7.4 Langton Cross

Satnav: Near Langton Herring, Dorset DT3 4HU (approx)

The B3157 is a busy road running out of Weymouth towards Portesham and Bridport. At one time a small mediaeval cross marked the turning to the village of Langton Herring, but over time this has become almost completely lost in the undergrowth. If you want to see the cross today, you will have to park in the layby next to the turning and go in search of it!

Langton Cross

According to legend, the cross comes to life once a year at midnight on New Year's Eve, at which time it travels a mile or so to the Fleet lagoon (see the item about the Bouncing Bomb in Chapter 8: *Weird Science*). It then anoints its head with water before returning to its normal place!

7.5 The Angels of Muchelney

Satnav: Muchelney, Somerset TA10 0DQ (Abbey is English Heritage)

Before the dissolution of the monasteries in the 16th century, Muchelney Abbey was the second largest monastic establishment in Somerset, after Glastonbury (see Chapter 1: *Weird Archaeology*). Since that time, like Glastonbury, Muchelney Abbey has largely fallen into ruin, although two of its buildings remain intact. One of these is the Abbot's House, the other is the large, thatched reredorter – or monks' lavatory! It is believed to be the only thatched communal toilet in Britain.

Muchelney Abbey

Muchelney's parish church of St Peter and St Paul is next door to the Abbey. It was built in the 15th century, but the colourful paintings of angels on the ceiling were added in the early 1600s. This was one of the most puritanical periods in English history, yet in spite of that some of Muchelney's angels are depicted with bare breasts!

Weird Religion

The ceiling of Muchelney church

Close-up of exhibitionist angels

7.6 The Meditation Chair

Satnav: Bishops Cannings, Wiltshire SN10 2JZ

Bishops Cannings is a village in Wiltshire, a short drive north-east of Devizes. The village church of St Mary the Virgin is believed to have been built in the second half of the 12th century, and gradually augmented and improved over the years. At some point during this lengthy history the church became home to a very peculiar chair.

The chair in question has a "Hand of Meditation" painted on its back. The hand is decorated with a number of depressing Latin phrases, presumably designed to make whoever is sitting in the chair consider their actions and the meaning of their life.

The Meditation Chair

According to the inscription accompanying the Hand of Meditation:

> *The origin of this ancient pew is uncertain. It is thought by some to be a confessional; by others a monastic carrel or study desk. Only the painted panel is mediaeval and belongs to the 15th century. The surrounding woodwork seems to have been added in the 18th century.*

The Latin inscriptions can apparently be translated as follows:

On the palm: *"What thou oughtest to think upon."*

On the thumb: *"Thou knowest not how much. Thou knowest not how often. Thou hast offended God."*

On the index finger: *"Thy end is bitter. Thy life is short. Thou hast come into the world with sin."*

On the middle finger: *"Thou shalt carry nothing with thee but what thou hast done. Thy life thou canst not lengthen. Thy death thou canst not escape. Thou shalt die."*

On the fourth finger: *"Thou knowest not whither thou shalt go. Thou knowest not how thou shalt die. Thou knowest not where thou shalt die. The hour of death is uncertain."*

On the little finger: *"Thou shalt quickly be forgotten by thy friends. Thy best will seldom do anything for thee. He to whom thou leaveth thy goods will seldom do anything for thee. Thy end is miserable."*

The Hand of Meditation

7.7 Martin's Ape

Satnav: St Bartholomew's church, Crewkerne, Somerset TA18 7HY

The parish church of Crewkerne in Somerset dates from the 15th century, but its most unusual feature is a small brass plaque commemorating Adam Martin of Seaborough, who died in 1678. The plaque, which can be found on the wall inside the church just to the right of the main west door, shows a chained monkey looking at itself in a mirror.

The Crewkerne monkey

The same image can be seen in other churches in the local area, though this is one of the clearest and earliest examples. The mirror-holding monkey was the mascot of the Martin (or Martyn) family, whose motto was *"He who looks at Martyn's ape, Martyn's ape shall look at him."*

The Crewkerne monkey became briefly famous in the 1890s, when it was used as an advertisement for "Monkey Brand" metal polish – though in that case, the monkey was looking at a reflection of himself in a highly polished frying pan!

7.8 The Nether Wallop Pyramid

Satnav: St Andrew's church, Nether Wallop, Hampshire SO20 8EY

Nether Wallop is a village in Hampshire, nine miles south-west of Andover. The village church is dedicated to St Andrew, and the churchyard is home to an intriguing fifteen foot tall stone pyramid. This unusual memorial marks a vaulted burial chamber known as the "Douce Mausoleum". This Grade II listed structure was built for the physician Dr Francis Douce (1675-1760) in 1748 and was designed by John Blake of Winchester. The pinnacle of the pyramid is capped off with a flaming torch, and one side of the pyramid bears a tablet which holds a coat of arms and an inscription.

The Nether Wallop pyramid

The Douce Mausoleum is not St Andrew's only unusual feature. The church itself contains the remains of frescoes, or wall paintings, the earliest of which – *Christ in Majesty* – is believed to date from the late Anglo-Saxon period. This Anglo-Saxon fresco is believed to be the only wall painting of the period to survive in situ, and is painted in the style of the "Winchester School" of manuscript illuminators who worked around the year 1020. The frescoes inside the church include:

Christ in Majesty: It seems that in late Saxon times that it was customary to depict "Christ in Majesty" over the chancel arch of a church, and the example in St Andrews church is estimated to date from 1025. The original St Andrews "Christ in Majesty" was a depiction of a seated Christ, with his right hand raised in benediction, and surrounded by a host of angels adorned with halos. Today the bottom two angels are still visible, but the centre part of the fresco has been destroyed. This is believed to have occurred in Norman times, when the chancel arch was widened.

The Sabbath Breakers: This is a 15th century morality painting depicting the potential dangers of breaking the fourth commandment: *"Remember the Sabbath day, and keep it holy..."* The fresco shows Christ who has been injured by a number of wounds. Christ is surrounded by the implements of different trades, including a plough, a millwright's tools, a cobbler's awl and knife, a slater's zax, a trader's scales, a saw, a bobbin of yarn, an axe, a catapult, a net, and a horseshoe. These tools are presumably the source of Christ's wounds, as the tradesmen who own them had been working on the Sabbath day.

St George and the Dragon: This fresco, probably dating from the 15th century, shows St George mounted on his horse fighting the Dragon outside the gates of a settlement, whilst two crowned figures (presumably a King and a Queen) look on.

St George and the Dragon

7.9 Portesham's Inside-Out Tomb

Satnav: St Peter's church, Portesham, Dorset DT3 4HB

Visitors to a village church expect to see tombs – either inside the church itself, for the more prestigious residents, or in the churchyard outside for the ordinary villagers. But the Dorset village of Portesham is unusual in having a tomb attached to the outside wall of the church.

This "inside-out" tomb belongs to a local farmer named William Weare, who died in 1670. For some mysterious reason, he is said to have stipulated that he should be buried *"neither inside nor outside the church"*... and this was the solution his family came up with!

William Weare's tomb

7.10 The Virgin Crowns

Satnav: Abbotts Ann, Hampshire SP11 7BE (approx)

St Mary's church in Abbotts Ann, near Andover in Hampshire, has an unusual claim to fame. As the information board inside the church states:

> Abbotts Ann remains the only parish in England which perpetuates this mediaeval custom of awarding Virgin's Crowns. The ceremony of this ancient burial rite takes place at the funeral of an unmarried person who was born, baptised, confirmed and died in the Parish of Abbotts Ann, and was a regular Communicant. Such persons must also be of unblemished reputation.

> The Virgin's Crown is made of Hazelwood and is ornamented with paper rosettes, with five white gauntlets attached to it. The gauntlets represent a challenge thrown down to anyone to asperse the character of the deceased. The Crown suspended from a rod is borne by two young girls habited in white with white hoods, at the head of the funeral procession. After the funeral the Crown [...] is hung in the roof of the Church with a small scutcheon bearing the name and age of the person concerned, and the date of her funeral, and there the Crown remains until it decays and falls with age.

> Most of the Crowns are awarded to women, but men are not excluded, provided that they fulfil the same conditions. The present Church was built in the year 1716 and the oldest Virgins Crown still in existence approaches that date.

Weird Religion

The crowns hanging inside the church

Today St Mary's church is home to a total of 49 Virgin's Crowns, honouring 15 men and 34 women. The oldest crown is dedicated to John Morrant who died in 1740. His crown has now entirely decayed and all that remains is the string from which it once hung. The newest crown dates from 1973 and is dedicated to Lily Myra Annetts who died aged 73. This crown seems to be wholly intact, with all five gauntlets still in place. The rest of the crowns are in various stages of decay, most with their gauntlets missing and many now blackened by the passage of time.

The oldest crown is second from left

the crowns hanging inside the church

The oldest crown is second from left

8 Weird Science

From fossil hunters and aviation pioneers to flying saucers and crop circles, Wessex has seen its fair share of weird science. The ten items in this chapter are arranged roughly in chronological order, starting with the age of the dinosaurs in Charmouth and the mediaeval proto-scientists of Malmesbury Abbey and Wimborne Minster. Then there is the monster-creator of Bournemouth, the aircraft-builder of Chard and the military boffins of Brean Down and Abbotsbury. Finally there are the latter-day fringe scientists of Wilsford-cum-Lake, Warminster and Honeystreet!

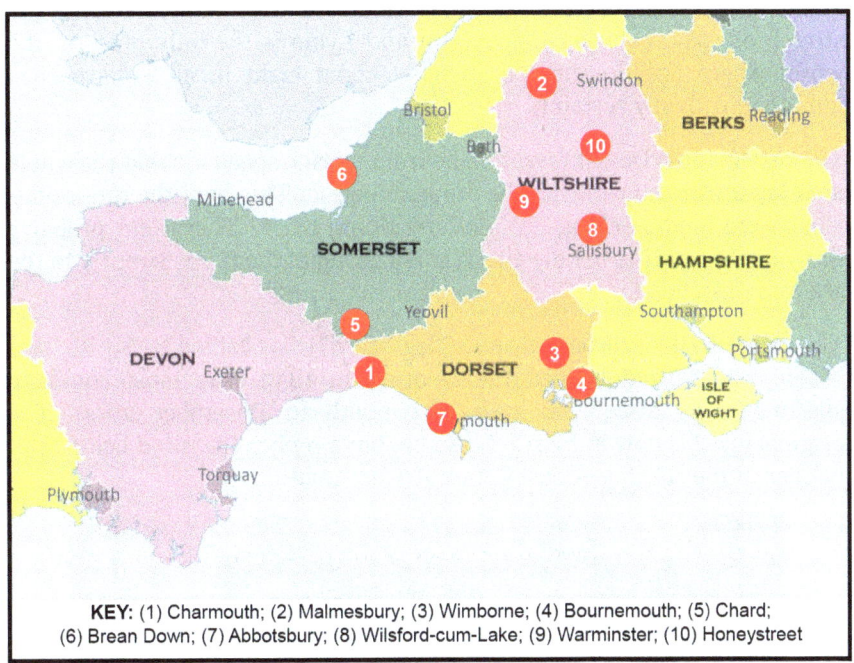

KEY: (1) Charmouth; (2) Malmesbury; (3) Wimborne; (4) Bournemouth; (5) Chard; (6) Brean Down; (7) Abbotsbury; (8) Wilsford-cum-Lake; (9) Warminster; (10) Honeystreet

Locator map for Weird Science

8.1 The Dorset Dinosaur

Satnav: Charmouth Heritage Coast Centre, Dorset DT6 6LR

The cliffs around Charmouth and Lyme Regis in Dorset are famous for their many fossils dating from the Jurassic period. To most people, the word "Jurassic" is synonymous with dinosaurs, but most of the Dorset fossils are marine animals rather than true dinosaurs. The most important exception is Scelidosaurus – Dorset's very own dinosaur.

Scelidosaurus was a large, armour-plated plant-eater similar in appearance to the better known Stegosaurus and Ankylosaurus. The stretch of coast between Charmouth and Lyme is the only place in the world where Scelidosaur specimens – about eight in all – have been identified with any certainty.

The reason most Dorset fossils come from marine species is that the whole area lay underwater during the Jurassic period. This begs the question – what were land-dwelling Scelidosaurs doing there? They were probably drowning! Scientists believe that a small group of them was swept into the sea by a flash flood.

The name Scelidosaurus (meaning "leg-lizard") was coined by Sir Richard Owen, who first described the creature in 1859. The most complete specimen was discovered near Charmouth in December 2000. The original fossil is now in Bristol Museum, but a replica (pictured below) can be seen at the Heritage Coast Centre in Charmouth.

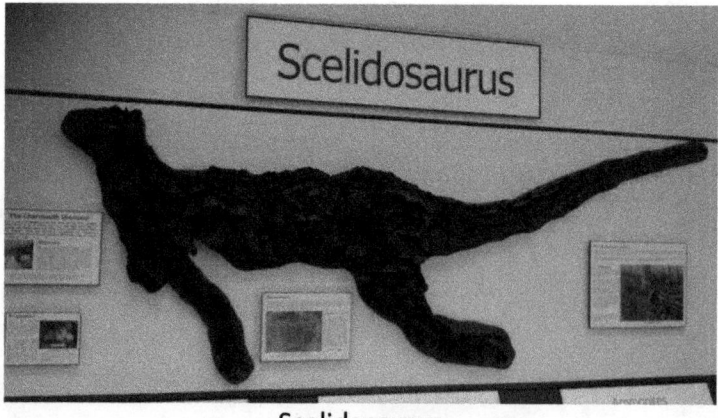

Scelidosaurus

8.2 The Flying Monk

Satnav: Malmesbury Abbey, Wiltshire SN16 9BA

Malmesbury Abbey in Wiltshire has a history reaching back to 676 AD, when a Benedictine monastery was first founded on the site. One of its more unusual claims to fame is Elmer the Flying Monk!

Malmesbury Abbey

Around 1125 the medieval historian William of Malmesbury wrote in his book *Gesta Regum Anglorum* (Deeds of the English Kings), about a monk from Malmesbury Abbey who is reputed to be Britain's first aviator. The monk's name was Elmer (sometimes spelled Eilmer), and it is said that around the year 1005 he managed to fly a distance of some 200 metres from the Abbey's tower using a rudimentary type of hang-glider. It seems that Elmer's flight was only a partial success. Although he did manage to glide, on landing he is said to have broken both his legs, leaving him lame for the rest of his days. In the 20th century Elmer was belatedly commemorated in a stained glass window in the Abbey, where he is depicted holding what appears to be a model of his hang-glider.

Elmer's window can be a little tricky to find, since it is not located in the main body of the Abbey but inside the crèche. If you turn left as you enter the Abbey you will find the crèche with Elmer's memorial window directly in front of you.

Elmer the flying monk (right)

Another unusual sight can be found in the graveyard at Malmesbury Abbey. This is the gravestone of Hannah Twynnoy, a barmaid at Malmesbury's White Lion Inn. One day in 1703 the pub was playing host to a travelling menagerie, when a tiger mauled the unfortunate Hannah to death. She is generally considered to be the first person to be killed by a tiger in Britain.

As you enter the Abbey's graveyard on the path that leads directly to the main door of the Abbey, Hannah's gravestone can be found set back from the path on the right hand side. The fading inscription reads:

In memory of
Hannah Twynnoy
who died October 23rd 1703
aged 33 years.

In bloom of Life she's snatch'd from hence,
She had not room to make defence;
For Tyger fierce took Life away.
And here she lies in a bed of Clay,
Until the Resurrection Day.

Hannah Twynnoy – killed by a tiger

8.3 Mediaeval Timekeeping

Satnav: Wimborne Minster, Dorset BH21 1EB

When the first mechanical clocks were made in the Middle Ages, it was still believed that the Sun revolved around the Earth once every 24 hours. This belief was reflected in the design of some early clocks, in which a representation of the Earth was placed at the centre of the clock face, and the hour hand was replaced by an "orbiting" model of the Sun. A good example of such a clock, dating from around 1320, can be seen inside the church of St Cuthberga in Wimborne Minster in Dorset.

Wimborne Minster's astronomical clock

The Earth is shown as a blue-green sphere at the very centre of the clock face. The Sun, which is a gold emblem painted on a black disc, revolves around the perimeter once every 24 hours, indicating the hour of the day as it orbits the Earth. Between the Earth and the Sun there is another sphere which has one hemisphere painted black, and the other gold. This represents the Moon, and correctly depicts the phases of the Moon as it orbits the Earth.

The Wimborne clock, dating from the early 14th century, is amongst the oldest working clocks in the world. Another clock of the same period and similar design, which may even have been made by the same person, can be seen in Wells Cathedral in Somerset. Devon's Exeter Cathedral also boasts an astronomical clock, although it is a later example, dating from circa 1484.

The Wells Cathedral clock

The Exeter Cathedral clock

8.4 Frankenstein's Creator

Satnav: St Peter's church, Bournemouth, Dorset BH1 2EE

Improbable as it sounds, the popular seaside resort of Bournemouth in Dorset is the last resting place of Mary Shelley, the author of *Frankenstein*. Her tomb can be found in St. Peter's churchyard near the centre of the town.

Mary Godwin was born in London in 1797, and married the poet Percy Bysshe Shelley in 1814 when she was just sixteen. Two years later, in the summer of 1816, she and Percy went to stay with Lord Byron at his villa near Lake Geneva. Unfortunately an ash cloud from a volcanic eruption in Indonesia had shrouded the entire northern hemisphere in darkness, forcing Mary and her friends to spend most of their time indoors. They amused themselves by writing ghosts stories, and it was during this dark and gloomy summer that the first version of *Frankenstein* was written.

Mary's husband Percy drowned in 1822 whilst out sailing off the Italian coast. His body was found on a beach 10 days later, and cremated nearby. When Mary herself died in 1851, a silk parcel was found among her possessions that appeared to contain some of Percy's ashes along with the remains of his heart – which according to legend refused to burn when he was cremated. Percy's incombustible heart was eventually interred along with Mary's remains in Bournemouth.

Mary Shelley's grave

8.5 Chard's Aviation Pioneer

Satnav: Chard, Somerset, TA20 1PP

According to the history books, the age of heavier-than-air powered aviation began with the Wright Brothers in 1903. But that was merely the first man-carrying flight. The first unmanned flight took place more than half a century earlier, in 1848, at Chard in Somerset.

The Stringfellow monument in Chard

John Stringfellow was born in Sheffield in 1799, moving to Chard at the age of 20 to work in a lacemaking factory there. But Stringfellow's interests ranged much wider than that. He experimented with electricity, studied ornithology and built miniature steam engines. Before long he teamed up with another skilful local inventor named William Henson. The two of them turned their attention to powered flying machines, envisioning a time when such vehicles would carry passengers around the world. However, their proposal for an "Aerial Transit Company" brought them nothing but ridicule.

Henson emigrated to America early in 1848, just a few months before Stringfellow finally achieved success. In June of that year, the world's first powered flight by a heavier-than-air vehicle took place in a disused lace factory in Chard. The small "drone" – to use the modern term – weighed nine pounds and had a ten-foot wingspan. It was powered by a small steam engine driving a pair of four-bladed propellers, and was launched from an inclined wire. After release the aircraft climbed towards an arrestor net designed to catch it at the other end of the hall. A few months later, Stringfellow repeated the experiment in front of a larger audience in London.

In later years Stringfellow built larger and more powerful models, including a 13-pound triplane with a one horsepower engine that was demonstrated at the Crystal Palace exhibition in 1868.

The Stringfellow monument is not the only oddity that can be seen in the town of Chard. In a quiet residential street there is a low but very thick concrete wall that serves no apparent purpose. It's screened from the road by a hedge, and most people probably go straight past without even noticing it. But the wall is massive enough to stop a fifty-tonne tank... which is exactly what it was designed to do. It was built at the start of the Second World War as part of the Taunton Stop Line, a defensive barrier similar in purpose to the GHQ Line (see Chapter 9: *Weird Secrets*). Chard's anti-tank wall is just one of many remnants of the Stop Line that can be seen to this day, but very few of them are in a town centre like this one.

The anti-tank wall in Chard

Weird Science

8.6 Brean Down Fort

Satnav: Brean Down, Somerset TA8 2RS (National Trust)

Brean Down is a promontory on the Somerset coast, a few miles south of Weston-Super-Mare. Overlooking the mouth of the Severn estuary, it has been a strategically important location since the Bronze Age. It was one of the sites chosen in the 1860s for the new tranche of anti-invasion defences known as Palmerston Forts (see the entry on Portsmouth in Chapter 3: *Weird Constructions*).

Brean Down Fort was completed in 1871, and remained in service for the rest of the 19th century. Its career came to an abrupt halt on 6 July 1900, when a gunner committed suicide by blowing himself up in the ammunition store!

The remains of Brean Down Fort

The site was recommissioned for military use at the outbreak of the Second World War in 1939, when it was rearmed with more modern guns. Its chief use during WW2 was as a test site for experimental naval weapons. One of the more unusual facilities at the site was a rocket-powered sled. This was designed to propel munitions into the sea at high speed, to simulate launch from a low-flying aircraft. The narrow-gauge trackway used by the sled can still been seen to this day.

The trackway at Brean Down

8.7 The Bouncing Bomb

Satnav: The Swannery, Abbotsbury, Dorset DT3 4JH (Admission charge)

The stretch of Dorset coast to the west of Weymouth is dominated by Chesil Beach, a long, straight barrier of shingle that was formed at the end of the last Ice Age, around 10,000 years ago. Between the beach and the mainland is a saltwater lagoon called the Fleet, which has become a haven for wading birds and other wildlife.

Chesil Beach and the Fleet

During the Middle Ages, the monks of Abbotsbury Abbey established a swannery – rearing swans as a food source in the way monks elsewhere might rear pigs or chickens. Although the monks are long gone, Abbotsbury Swannery is still there – run today as a tourist attraction rather than a livestock farm.

Abbotsbury Swannery

The peace and quiet of the Fleet was shattered during the Second World War when it was used by the Royal Air Force as an experimental bombing range. The most famous weapons to be tested there were the "bouncing bombs" designed by Sir Barnes Wallis. The Fleet – being a long, smooth stretch of water – was an ideal place to test such devices. Two different types of bouncing bomb were tested there between December 1942 and March 1943: a cylindrical design called Upkeep and a dimpled sphere called Highball. The tests showed that Upkeep was the more promising design, and it went on to be used in the famous "dambuster" raids of May 1943.

In 1992, an experimental version of the Highball bomb was recovered from the Fleet, which can now be seen on display at Abbotsbury Swannery. This was an inert prototype, filled with a mixture of concrete and cork to give it the same weight – one ton – that a live weapon would have.

Abbotsbury's Bouncing Bomb

8.8 A Pioneer of Psychical Research

Satnav: Wilsford-cum-Lake, Wiltshire SP4 7BL

The small village of Wilsford-cum-Lake in Wiltshire may have one of the rudest-sounding place names in the country (oo-er, missus!) but it has another even weirder claim to fame, as the last resting place of one of Britain's first paranormal investigators.

Wilsford-cum-Lake

The graveyard of St Michael's churchyard includes a tombstone with the following inscription:

> *Oliver Joseph Lodge*
> *Born 12 June 1851*
> *Died 22 August 1940*
> *Thankful For The Love Which Has*
> *Surrounded Him Throughout His*
> *Time On Earth Full of Certainty*
> *About Continued Existence*
> *And Hopeful That His Writings May*
> *Be A Comfort To The Bereaved*

Sir Oliver Joseph Lodge died near Wilsford-cum-Lake at the age of 90 in 1940. He was a professional scientist whose illustrious career included a professorship of Physics and Mathematics at Liverpool University, and being elected the first Principal of Birmingham University when it received its Royal Charter in 1900. Lodge's achievements resulted in him being knighted by King Edward VII and becoming a Fellow of the Royal

Society in 1902. Lodge's chief area of interest was electromagnetics, particularly in relation to the then fashionable theory of the Ether.

Outside his mainstream scientific studies, however, Lodge was also deeply interested in psychical phenomena. He studied telepathy, was a member of the Ghost Club and served as president of the Society for Psychical Research from 1901 to 1903. His acceptance of the theory of the Ether in a scientific context led him to speculate that the Ether may also be host to a spirit world. He pursued this idea after his youngest son, Raymond, was tragically killed during the First World War. Lodge visited mediums who claimed they could communicate with his dead son. His scientific background meant that he regularly tested the mediums and probed them for information that only his son would know, yet he failed to find any reason to disbelieve their claims. Lodge became convinced there was an afterlife, and in 1916 he published an account of his son's adventures in the spirit world called "Raymond, or Life and Death".

In a final attempt to prove the existence of an afterlife, Lodge deposited a sealed message with the Society for Psychical Research just before his death. His aim was to communicate the contents of this sealed message from the afterlife via a medium. Unfortunately however the results of Lodge's last experiment were inconclusive.

Gravestone of Sir Oliver Lodge

Weird Science

8.9 The Warminster Thing

Satnav: Cley Hill, Warminster, Wiltshire BA12 7QU (National Trust)

Cley Hill is a former Iron Age hill-fort about two miles west of Warminster. Evidence of the prehistoric earthworks can still be seen today, along with two Bronze Age round barrows. In recent times, however, Cley Hill – and Cradle Hill on the other side of Warminster – have become better known as places of pilgrimage for UFO spotters hoping to experience the "Warminster Thing".

Cley Hill

The story of the Warminster Thing began with strange noises being heard towards the end of 1964. These noises – which were described in various terms as "branches being pulled over gravel", "giant hailstones" and "rattling roof tiles" – were soon joined by strange objects seen in the sky. The first UFO reported hovering over Warminster was a silent cigar-shaped object covered in winking lights.

Following widespread news coverage of these events, Warminster quickly gained a reputation as a UFO hot spot. Sky-watchers flocked to Cley Hill and Cradle Hill to try to catch a glimpse of the "Thing". Popular interest in the Warminster mystery remained strong until the late 1970s, and even to this day some die-hard UFO buffs still visit the area every year to conduct sky-watches.

The mystery of what caused the strange sights and noises around Warminster has never been satisfactorily solved, although the town's proximity to the military training area on Salisbury Plain, and the RAF's test and evaluation airfield at Boscombe Down, may indicate a military origin for at least some of the phenomena.

To mark the 50th anniversary of the Warminster Thing, a mural was unveiled early in 2015 opposite the town's Tourist Information Centre. Partially painted in glow-in-the-dark colours, the mural depicts strange creatures and triangular UFOs hovering over the distinctive shape of Cley Hill.

The Warminster UFO mural

8.10 Crop Circle Country

Satnav: Honeystreet, Pewsey, Wiltshire SN9 5PS

Every year the Wiltshire countryside sees dozens, if not hundreds, of crop circles popping up overnight as if by magic. The bulk of these crop circles – or crop formations, as they are not always circular – tend to occur near ancient sites such as Stonehenge, Avebury, Silbury Hill and the various chalk hill figures which comprise the mystical landscape of Wiltshire.

The phenomenon of crop circles first came to prominence in the United Kingdom in the late 1970s. This new phenomenon soon caught the public's attention, and explanations ranged from extraterrestrial visitors to freak weather events such as tornadoes or ball lightning. The reality seems to be much more prosaic, however. In the early 1990s two artists from Southampton claimed to have created a significant number of the circles, using planks of wood, rope and a baseball cap fitted with a loop of wire. The latter was apparently designed to help them walk in straight lines. Today, most people accept that crop circles are the product of human ingenuity, rather than visiting aliens or rare atmospheric phenomenon.

The Barge Inn

Nevertheless crop circles retain their appeal, and every year people from around the world travel to Wiltshire to see the latest batch of circles. The hub of crop circle hunting in Wiltshire is the Barge Inn, located in Honeystreet on the Kennet and Avon Canal. The inn, dating from 1810, is positioned on the Duke's Ley Line which runs from Avebury to

Stonehenge. It is right at the centre of Wiltshire's mystical landscape, close to Britain's oldest road, the Ridgeway, and not far from the ancient complex of Avebury, which was described in Chapter 1 on *Weird Archaeology*. The Inn is also overlooked by the Alton Barnes White Horse and Adam's Grave Long Barrow, as featured in *Weird Landscape.*

The Barge Inn has a crop circle room, where an up-to-date record is kept of the current batch of crop formations, together with aerial photographs and a map showing their location. Each summer this room becomes the hub from which circle spotters set out to explore new formations as soon as they appear.

Information on the current batch of crop formations (summer 2014)

Other aspects of the mystical and unusual are also featured at the Barge Inn. The ceiling of the crop circle room has a detailed and exquisitely painted mural, showing the ancient Pagan sites that fill the nearby countryside. Some call this mural the "Sistine Chapel of Wiltshire". Taking the Pagan theme even further, the Inn hosts Handfasting ceremonies. During these ceremonies couples can pledge their love for each other by the ceremonial binding of hands. The practice of Handfasting originates from an old Norse custom, and the Norse term "hand-festa" means "to strike a bargain by joining hands".

The Barge Inn doesn't neglect its primary function, either. Visitors can partake in numerous suitably named beverages, such as Croppie Ale, Area 51 Cider, Alien Abduction Green Ale, and Roswell Ale. The Inn is currently seeking planning permission to erect an observatory in its grounds, which would enable customers at the bar to keep an eye on the stars and watch out for incoming flying saucers!

9 Weird Secrets

The previous chapters have already uncovered quite a few "weird secrets", but here are ten more. They have been arranged in three thematic groups – the abandoned villages of Imber, Tyneham and Sutton Bingham, the historic secrets of Beer Quarry Caves and Dunster Castle, and the military secrets of the GHQ Line, Portland's Verne Citadel, Grovely Wood and the Royal Signals Museum... all rounded off with the grave of James Bond's creator, Ian Fleming!

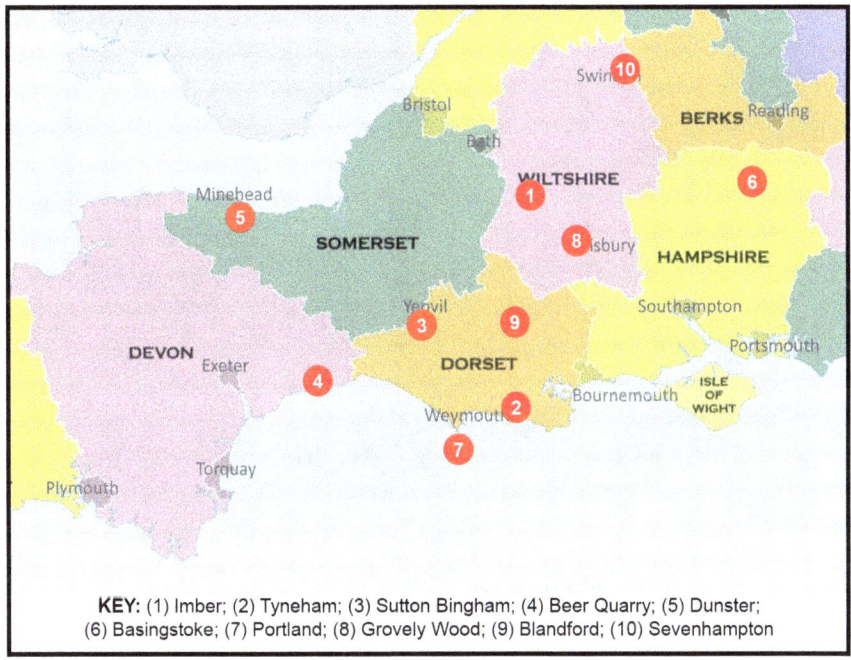

KEY: (1) Imber; (2) Tyneham; (3) Sutton Bingham; (4) Beer Quarry; (5) Dunster; (6) Basingstoke; (7) Portland; (8) Grovely Wood; (9) Blandford; (10) Sevenhampton

Locator map for Weird Secrets

9.1 Ghost Town

**Postcode: Imber village, Wiltshire SN10 4NG
(access limited to a few days per year)**

The abandoned village of Imber in Wiltshire is one of the most inaccessible places in England, locked away for most of the year inside the British Army's training grounds. The last week of August is one of the few times the village is open to the public.

Imber

Imber was always an isolated place, even when it was lived in:

> *Seven miles from any town,*
> *There stands Imber on the Down.*

Nevertheless, Imber existed as a small populated settlement for about a thousand years, the first documented mention of the village occurring in 967 AD. At the time of the Domesday book, compiled in 1086, the population was around 50 persons, rising to around 250 during the 14th century. The population was recorded as 440 in the census of 1851, but had declined to about 150 by the time Imber was abandoned during the Second World War.

Weird Secrets

In November 1943, while the Allied forces were making preparations for the D-Day landings, the residents of Imber were called to a meeting in the village schoolroom and told they had 47 days to leave their homes. The Army wanted to use the village to practice urban warfare prior to the invasion of Normandy. The villagers left their homes with no resistance, having been assured they could return when the war was over. But that was not to be – the Army continues to use Imber for urban warfare training to this day.

Imber Court

Imber's buildings are now empty shells

9.2 The Deserted Village

Satnav: Tyneham village, Dorset BH20 5DE (approx)

Tyneham in Dorset, like Imber in Wiltshire, is another village that has been abandoned since the Second World War. Public access to Tyneham is slightly easier than Imber, though. It is part of the Army's Lulworth Ranges, which are open most weekends, as well as the whole of August and over the Christmas holiday period.

The village of Tyneham, together with the surrounding area, was appropriated by the Army in 1943 as an artillery firing range. As in the case of Imber, this was originally pitched to the locals as a temporary measure for the duration of the war… but, as with Imber, the site remains in Army hands to this day.

Tyneham village

Although Tyneham has a similar history to Imber, its atmosphere is completely different. There are nothing like as many warning signs, and all the buildings in the village are open to the public. Unlike Imber, where the houses are kept in good repair for use in urban warfare training, Tyneham's buildings have been allowed to fall into picturesque decay. The location of Tyneham is more scenic, too, being less than a mile from Dorset's Jurassic Coast. A public footpath leads to Worbarrow Bay, which is also part of the Army ranges and has a small abandoned settlement of its own.

One of Tyneham's deserted buildings

Worbarrow Bay

9.3 The Artificial Lake

Satnav: Sutton Bingham Reservoir, Somerset BA22 9QP

Sutton Bingham was a small village near Yeovil whose fortunes peaked in the 19th century when, for a brief time, it got its own railway station on the London to Exeter line. Even in those days, however, its population was only around 80 people. By the 1950s the village had shrunk so much that Yeovil council was able to buy up all the remaining properties and use the land to construct a new reservoir. Most of what remained of the village, including Sutton Mill, was soon lost to sight beneath what is effectively a huge artificial lake. As well as being used as Yeovil's main water source, the reservoir is home to a nature reserve and a sailing club.

Sutton Bingham reservoir

One of the few remaining buildings that can still be seen above water is the small church of All Saints, dating from the Norman period. The church is notable for containing a number of mediaeval wall paintings, which were whitewashed over during the Reformation and only rediscovered in Victorian times (unfortunately however there is no public access to the interior of the church).

Weird Secrets

Another view of the reservoir

The Norman church

9.4 Beer Quarry Caves

Satnav: Beer Quarry Caves, Devon EX12 3AT (admission charge)

Beer is a small seaside village on the south coast of Devon. A short distance inland is a tourist attraction somewhat misleadingly known as "Beer Quarry Caves". These aren't natural caves, though, but artificial workings – and they're more reminiscent of a mine than a quarry.

There are no surface workings at Beer Quarry – just miles and miles of man-made tunnels. So why is it called a quarry and not a mine? Technically, a mine is a place for extracting minerals, whereas what was extracted from the ground here was stone – a special kind of limestone called Beer Stone. This has been in demand as a building material since the time of the Romans, who first started tunnelling here in the 1st century AD. After that the quarry was worked for almost 2000 years, with just a short break in the 16th and 17th centuries, before finally being closed down early in the 20th century.

Inside Beer Quarry Caves

Most limestone is either too soft to use as a structural material, or so hard that it is difficult to carve into intricate shapes. That was a big problem in the Middle Ages, when everyone wanted to build ornate churches and cathedrals out of stone. Beer Stone offered the best of both worlds. In its natural, waterlogged state it is easy to work into any shape, since it's very fine grained. Then when it dries out it becomes as hard as the hardest Portland stone. Not only was Beer Stone used in constructing the nearby cathedral at Exeter, but also much further afield at Winchester Cathedral, Westminster Abbey and even the Tower of London.

The heyday of Beer Quarry was the great age of church building in the 13th to 15th centuries. All this came to an abrupt end with the English Reformation in the 1530s, which proved to be a disastrous time for the quarrying industry. It wasn't just that work on church building came to an end, but the demolition of all the monasteries meant that millions of tonnes of ready-worked stone suddenly came onto the market for use in non-religious buildings.

During the enforced hiatus in quarrying at Beer, other more clandestine uses were found for the caves. When Catholic church services were made illegal, on punishment of death, they were driven underground... literally. Part of the tunnel network was converted into a chapel, the empty shell of which can still be seen today. The other clandestine use of the mine was for storing smuggler's contraband. It was ideal for this purpose, partly because of its close proximity to the sea and partly because of the vast and confusing network of pitch-dark tunnels.

The "Chapel" in Beer Quarry Caves

9.5 Dunster Castle

Satnav: Dunster Castle, Somerset TA24 6SL (National Trust)

Dunster is a small village about three miles from Minehead on the north Somerset coast. The castle overlooking the village was built soon after the Norman conquest in the 11th century, by a powerful Norman baron named William de Mohun. He soon acquired a reputation as the Scourge of the West:

> *From the fair and strong castle of Dunster, in which he had assembled a considerable body of knights and soldiers, he laid waste and plundered the surrounding country far and near, putting to the sword, carrying off and burning all and everything offering resistance, and inflicting tortures on those who were suspected of possessing wealth.*

Dunster Castle remained in the de Mohun family until the end of the 14th century, when it was sold to another Anglo-Norman family, the Luttrells. Succeeding generations of this family lived in the castle until 1976, when it passed to the National Trust.

Dunster Castle

Present-day visitors to Dunster Castle can discover one of its more interesting secrets. During the English Civil War, the Luttrells remained loyal to King Charles I in his struggle against the Parliamentarians. In May

1645, the King dispatched his 15-year old son – the future Charles II – to Dunster Castle in an attempt to boost the morale of local Royalists. The young prince spent a fortnight in the castle – in a room with its own secret passage, just in case the enemy turned up unexpectedly!

Interior of Dunster Castle, with portrait of a Civil War cavalier

9.6 The GHQ Line

Satnav: Crookham Village, Hampshire GU51 5SD (approx)

At the start of the Second World War, fears of a German invasion were such that a series of defences were built across the country. One of the most extensive schemes was known as the General Headquarters (GHQ) Line. This spanned a number of counties and was aimed at slowing down any invasion and preventing German soldiers and tanks from making inroads from the south coast.

One of the more scenic places to explore the remains of the GHQ Line is along the towpath of the Basingstoke canal, walking westwards from Crookham Village in Hampshire. A number of different types of defences can be seen along the way, ranging from pillboxes to tank traps. The following pictures show just a few examples, in sequence moving westwards along the canal.

Anti-tank defences in the form of "dragon's teeth" – pyramid-shaped concrete blocks deployed to impede the movement of tanks and other vehicles:

Dragon's teeth

Reinforced concrete cylinders, which, like the dragon's teeth, were primarily put in place to slow down the advance of tanks and other vehicles:

Concrete road blocks

Type 24 pillbox, shaped like an irregular hexagon, and designed to protect gun crews:

Type 24 pillbox

A different design of pillbox, square in shape:

Square pillbox

Concrete sockets to hold anti-vehicle mines:

Sockets for mines

9.7 The Verne Citadel

Satnav: The Verne, Portland, Dorset DT5 1EQ

The Isle of Portland in Dorset was another area, along with Portsmouth (see Chapter 3: *Weird Constructions*) and Brean Down (see Chapter 8: *Weird Science*) that was fortified with "Palmerston's Follies" against a French invasion in the 1860s.

The most ambitious of the Portland defences is the Verne Citadel, located 500 feet above sea level at the highest point of the island. This has been a strategically important site since the time of the Romans, who built their own fort there. Its Victorian successor, which can be seen to this day, is a monumental edifice – 56 acres in area, surrounded by a deep moat and designed to house a thousand troops. In its heyday in the 19th century it was armed with heavy artillery pointing out to sea on three sides, but during the 20th century the building was converted for use as a prison. It is now a detention centre for illegal immigrants.

The Verne Citadel

The Verne was built from local Portland stone – an important building material that was also used in Buckingham Palace and St Paul's Cathedral in London. In the case of the Verne, even though the stone didn't have far to travel, a huge amount of it was needed. The free-standing rock pillar known as Nicodemus Knob shows the extent of the quarrying that was required – all the surrounding stone was cut away for use in building the Verne Citadel.

Nicodemus Knob

Another former military "secret", located just a few hundred metres from the Verne, is Portland's High Angle Battery. This was built around 1892, as additional protection for ships in Portland Harbour. The battery is not visible from the sea, giving it an element of surprise – the 9 inch shells were fired upwards at a high angle so as to fall down onto the decks of unsuspecting enemy vessels. The battery also incorporates an underground laboratory, a large bombproof shelter and a network of tunnels – the latter reportedly harbouring a number of ghosts!

The High Angle Battery

9.8 The Bunker in the Woods

Satnav: Grovely Wood, Wiltshire SP3 4SQ

During the Cold War, Wiltshire became closely linked in the popular imagination with tales of "secret underground bunkers". While some of these were nothing more than urban legends, others were undoubtedly real, such as the Burlington Bunker (a.k.a. the Central Government War Headquarters) near Corsham. Wiltshire is far enough from London to be relatively "safe" from nuclear bombs, but close enough that senior members of the government could get there in a hurry if they needed to.

At least one bunker in Wiltshire is far from secret, however. It is located in Grovely Wood, a few miles north-east of Salisbury, and – these days at least – it is conveniently labelled with the word "Bunker". This one doesn't date from the Cold War, though, but from the Second World War. It appears to be an air-raid shelter of the Stanton type, and can be found alongside the old Roman road running through the centre of the woods. Oakley Farm nearby served as an RAF Ordnance Depot and headquarters during the war, while Grovely Wood itself was used by the US Air Force as an ammunition depot.

The Grovely Wood bunker

Grovely Wood hides another, more grisly secret too. The ancient woodland is associated with a gruesome multiple murder which is supposed to have occurred in 1737. That year, four Danish sisters named Handsel moved into the area. Unfortunately their arrival coincided with an outbreak of smallpox, resulting in the deaths of 132 local people. The survivors, believing the sisters were witches who were responsible for the disease, took them to Grovely Wood and bludgeoned them to death.

The sisters are supposedly buried in the woods in four separate graves, said to be marked by four gnarled beech trees. Three of these "Handsel" trees are still standing, and the largest of them has a hollow at its base where people still leave offerings to the murdered sisters.

The largest of the Handsel Trees, with a hollow at its base

Weird Secrets

9.9 Royal Signals Museum

**Satnav: Royal Signals Museum, Blandford Camp, Dorset DT11 8RH
(admission charge)**

The Royal Signals Museum in Dorset is one of the country's most secure tourist attractions. Located inside an Army base, visitors have to pass through military-style security screening in order to enter the site. A photo ID is essential – preferably a passport – and exterior photography is not permitted. Once inside the museum, however, you can take whatever photographs you like.

The museum is devoted to all the most secret aspects of warfare. It traces the evolution of British special forces from the Long Range Desert Group of the Second World War to today's SAS. Its displays include concealed electronic equipment used by spies, resistance fighters and prisoners of war. All aspects of electronic warfare are covered, from eavesdropping and signal interception to cryptography – including the work of the Bletchley Park codebreakers of WW2 – and modern cyber warfare of the digital age.

A German Enigma Machine from WW2

9.10 The Man who Created James Bond

Satnav: Sevenhampton, Wiltshire SN6 7QA

James Bond must be Britain's best-known secret agent, albeit a fictional one. But Bond's creator, Ian Fleming, really did work in military intelligence during the Second World War. When he wrote the James Bond novels, beginning with *Casino Royale* in 1953, he was drawing on his own real-life experiences.

The eighth novel in the series, *Thunderball*, was based on a screenplay Fleming had written in collaboration with two other authors. This resulted in a lengthy court case, the stress of which caused Fleming to suffer a heart attack in April 1961. He recovered enough to write four more novels, but before he had time to put the final touches on the last of these – *The Man with the Golden Gun* – he suffered as second heart attack, on 11 August 1964, and died the following day. His grave can be found in the churchyard at Sevenhampton, a small village about five miles north-east of Swindon.

Ian Fleming's grave

10 Weird Tales

From larger-than-life figures like Sir Walter Raleigh and Lawrence of Arabia to the inspiration behind Robinson Crusoe, Sherlock Holmes and the Lord of the Rings, the Wessex region has plenty of Weird Tales to offer. The ten items in this chapter – all interesting tourist destinations in their own right – are arranged chronologically. From the 16th century we have Sherborne's Raleigh connection, while the 18th century provides Somerset's links to Robinson Crusoe and the Ancient Mariner. The 20th century gives us the Hound of the Baskervilles (Dartmoor), a sleazy lady novelist (Montacute), the home of T.E. Lawrence (Cloud's Hill), the curse of the Pharaoh (Highclere Castle), one of Agatha Christie's greatest mysteries (Burgh Island), Tolkien's ring (The Vyne) and even a classic Doctor Who setting (Winspit Quarry).

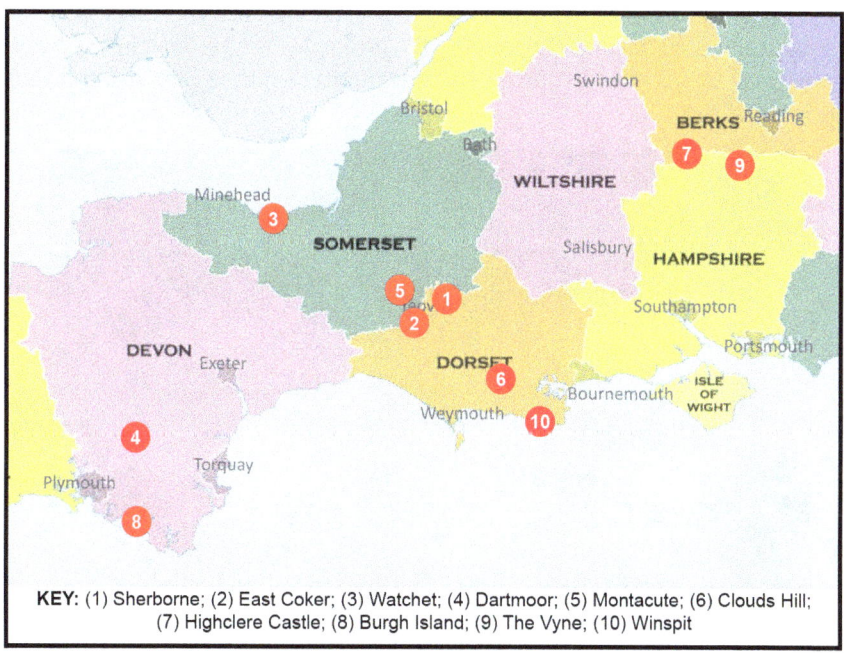

Locator map for Weird Tales

10.1 Sherborne Castles

Satnav: Sherborne Old Castle, Dorset DT9 3SA (English Heritage)

The town of Sherborne in Dorset has two castles, both of which have strong associations with the Elizabethan adventurer Sir Walter Raleigh. Best known as the person who first introduced tobacco to England from the New World, Raleigh was the archetypal Renaissance Man – explorer, poet, politician and spy! At the age of just 30, in 1585, he was knighted by Queen Elizabeth I and went on to become one of her closest advisors. Subsequently, however, he fell from favour and was executed by King James I in 1618.

The Old Castle at Sherborne was built in the 12th century, and was still more or less intact in Raleigh's time. In those days, the main route from the capital in London to the country's principal international port at Plymouth ran right past the castle, and Raleigh became fascinated by it. He expressed his admiration to the queen, and in 1592 she granted him the lease of the castle.

Sherborne Old Castle

Initially, Raleigh set to work refurbishing the Old Castle in an attempt to bring it up to the standards of the 16th century. But this proved harder than anticipated, so he built a brand new "castle" a short distance away.

The old castle gradually became a picturesque ruin, which is still there to this day. It is currently owned by English Heritage and open to the public. The New Castle is privately owned, but is also open to visitors.

Another view of Sherborne Old Castle

Sherborne New Castle

10.2 An Explorer and a Poet

Satnav: East Coker church, Somerset BA22 9JW

The village of East Coker near Yeovil in Somerset has two completely different claims to literary fame, both commemorated by plaques in the church of St Michael.

East Coker church

The village's most famous resident was the explorer William Dampier, who circumnavigated the world three times in the late 17th and early 18th century. After his first circumnavigation he wrote a book, *A New Voyage Round the World*, which was an instant bestseller and made him the talk of London society. It is not the most famous book associated with Dampier, though.

On a later voyage he was forced to deal with a near-mutiny caused by a cantankerous quartermaster named Alexander Selkirk. Dampier ended up marooning Selkirk on an uninhabited island off the coast of South America – where the man remained for four years until Dampier finally came back to retrieve him. A fictionalized version of Selkirk's story was later published by Daniel Defoe under the title *Robinson Crusoe*.

Plaque commemorating William Dampier

East Coker's other literary connection comes through an American, T.S. Eliot, who was one of the most important avant-garde poets of the 20th century. Eliot's ancestors originally came from East Coker, and he used the name of the village as the title of a poem he wrote in 1940.

Plaque commemorating T.S. Eliot

10.3 The Ancient Mariner

Satnav: Watchet, Somerset TA23 0DG

The town of Watchet on the north coast of Somerset has a rather bizarre-looking statue, depicting a man with a dead albatross hanging around his neck. This is a reference to the famous "horror poem" *The Rime of the Ancient Mariner*, written by Samuel Taylor Coleridge in 1798.

The Ancient Mariner

Coleridge was born in Ottery St Mary in Devon, but spent some of his most productive years in North Somerset. Between 1797 and 1799 he lived in Nether Stowey, in what is now known as Coleridge Cottage – a National Trust property which is open to the public. It was here that he wrote *The Ancient Mariner*, and also the partly completed fragment known as *Kubla Khan*. The latter came to Coleridge in a "pipe dream" after smoking opium, and he began to write it down as soon as he awoke. However, he was interrupted by a "person from Porlock" and was unable to remember the rest of the poem after the unwelcome visitor had left.

Coleridge Cottage in Nether Stowey

10.4 Dartmoor

Satnav: Dartmoor Visitor Centre, Princetown, Devon PL20 6QF

The Dartmoor National Park in Devon is one of England's bleakest landscapes. Its rocky terrain is the largest area of granite in the country, more than 200 square miles in extent. Despite its enormous size, Dartmoor only has a few thousand human inhabitants – and the less fortunate of those are securely locked up in the prison at the heart of the moor.

Dartmoor Prison, constructed from local granite, is situated just outside the small settlement of Princetown. It was originally built early in the 19th century as a repository for French and American military prisoners (Britain was at war with both countries at the time). Later in the 19th century it was converted to a civilian prison, and by the 20th century it had a reputation as one of the most secure in the country.

The entrance to Dartmoor Prison

The combination of Dartmoor's bleak landscape and high-security prison made it an attractive setting for writers of mystery fiction. It features prominently in *The Sittaford Mystery*, a crime novel – with hints of the supernatural – by Agatha Christie, as well as Arthur Conan Doyle's short story "Silver Blaze", featuring his world-famous detective Sherlock Holmes. But the ultimate Dartmoor-based "weird tale" must be the Sherlock Holmes novel *The Hound of the Baskervilles*. One of Doyle's best-known works, this was originally published in 1902. Although a work of fiction, *The Hound of the Baskervilles* was inspired by longstanding legends of a spectral hound that is supposed to haunt the moor.

Typical Dartmoor landscape

10.5 Montacute House

Satnav: Montacute House, Somerset TA15 6XP (National Trust)

Montacute House in South Somerset was built in the late Elizabethan period, around 1598. It is a prime example of the renaissance style, and unusual among English houses in following the continental practice of adorning the exterior with statues – in this case, an array of historic figures from Alexander the Great and Julius Caesar to King Arthur and Charlemagne.

Some of the historic figures at Montacute House

The original owner of Montacute was Sir Edward Phelips, who became a senior member of the government under King James I. The house remained in the Phelips family until the early 20th century, when dwindling funds and increased maintenance costs forced them to vacate the property and lease it to tenants.

The most famous of Montacute's tenants was Lord Curzon, a member of a wealthy Derbyshire family, who used the house as a second home between 1915 and his death in 1925. Curzon's place in history rests on the fact that he was Britain's foreign secretary immediately after the First World War.

One of his tasks was to establish a new boundary between Poland and the Soviet Union, which became known as the "Curzon Line".

Lord Curzon, however, is not as interesting as the reason he needed to rent Montacute as a second home. That reason was a woman named Elinor Glyn, who wasn't Lord Curzon's wife.

Elinor Glyn was a prolific novelist who specialized in a rather sleazy form of literature. She was one of the first writers to discover the huge and previously untapped market among female readers for "erotic romance". Her works were tame by modern standards, but in her day they were as talked-about as *Fifty Shades of Grey* is today. Elinor acquired worldwide notoriety both as a scandalous author, and as a scandalously seductive beauty. Lord Curzon was one of the many men who fell for her charms, and in 1906 he started an affair with her which lasted ten years.

When Lord Curzon moved to Montacute in 1915, he asked Elinor to oversee its redecoration. No expense was spared, with silk hangings on the walls, specially commissioned furniture, and tiger skins on the floor. In fact a tiger skin was the scene of some of the "action" in Elinor's most notorious novel, *Three Weeks* – a scene which became so famous it inspired the following ditty:

> *Would you like to sin with Elinor Glyn*
>   *On a tiger skin?*
> *Or would you prefer to err with her*
>   *On some other fur?*

Elinor hoped that Lord Curzon would eventually marry her, but to her dismay he became engaged to another woman at the end of 1916. She promptly packed her bags and left Montacute, never to return.

Modern-day visitors to Montacute House can see Lord Curzon's bedroom, complete with central heating and en-suite bath. The room contains plenty of reminders of Elinor's presence at Montacute, including a portrait of her and a selection of her novels.

10.6 Lawrence of Arabia

Satnav: Clouds Hill, Wareham, Dorset BH20 7NQ (National Trust)

After the First World War, the British soldier T. E. Lawrence wrote *The Seven Pillars of Wisdom*, a dramatic account of his exploits during the Middle East campaign of that conflict. These exploits were subsequently brought to a wider audience in the 1962 blockbuster movie, *Lawrence of Arabia*.

Lawrence left military service at the age of 46 in 1935, and retired to a tiny, isolated cottage in rural Dorset called Clouds Hill. This cottage is now owned by the National Trust, and kept much as it was when Lawrence lived there. Visitors get a strong impression both of Lawrence's eccentrically austere lifestyle, and his passion for the Middle East.

Clouds Hill

Two months after his retirement, Lawrence was killed in a motorcycle accident as he was on his way back to Clouds Hill from a post office about a mile away. As he came up out of a dip in the road he suddenly found himself behind two teenage boys on push bikes. He swerved to miss them, but was flung head-first over the handlebars of his own motorbike.

Lawrence wasn't wearing a crash helmet, and he suffered severe head injuries which resulted in his death six day later on 19 May 1935. He was buried in the cemetery at Moreton, about a mile and a half south-west of Clouds Hill.

Lawrence of Arabia's grave

The circumstances of Lawrence's death have been complicated by the testimony of one of the witnesses who gave evidence at the inquest, Corporal Ernest Catchpole. He claimed to have been following a hundred yards behind Lawrence, and to have seen a large black car coming in the opposite direction just before the crash. According to Catchpole's version of events, it was this vehicle, and not the push bikes, that caused Lawrence's fatal swerve. This has led some conspiracy theorists to suggest that – as with similar theories of the death of Diana, Princess of Wales – the "accident" was deliberately caused by person or persons unknown.

10.7 The Mummy's Curse

Satnav: Highclere Castle, Berkshire RG20 9RN

Highclere Castle, about five miles south of Newbury in Berkshire, is the ancestral home of the Earls of Carnarvon. The most famous member of the family was the 5th Earl, who was the wealthy sponsor behind Howard Carter's excavations of Tutankhamun's tomb in the Valley of the Kings. He was also one of the first people to fall victim to the so-called "Mummy's curse".

Highclere Castle

Lord Carnarvon was a keen amateur Egyptologist who sponsored digs in Egypt as early as 1907. In 1914 he received permission to dig in the Valley of the Kings, where the historic discovery was made in November 1922. When Carnarvon and Carter uncovered the tomb of Tutankhamun, it had lain undisturbed and intact for nearly 3000 years, and was found to be packed full with a wealth of ancient artefacts.

Carnarvon's public renown did not end with the discovery of Tutankhamun's tomb. Ironically, his death in Cairo on the 5th April 1923 – just a few months later – also helped to make his name widely known. On 19th March of that year Carnarvon suffered a severe mosquito bite, which subsequently became infected following a razor cut. This infection led to his death from suspected blood poisoning, and kick-started the legend of the "Mummy's Curse" surrounding the excavation of Tutankhamun's tomb.

The tomb of the 5th Earl of Carnarvon can be seen on Beacon Hill, a former Iron Age hill-fort overlooking Highclere Castle. The hill derives its name from the fact that it was once used as the site of one of Hampshire's many signalling beacons.

Lord Carnarvon's Tomb

Highclere Castle itself sits amidst impressive grounds which are home to a number of interesting follies, including a Temple of Diana dating from around 1743, and Heaven's Gate, built a few years later in 1749.

The Temple of Diana

10.8 Mystery Island

Satnav: Bigbury-on-Sea, Devon TQ7 4AZ

Burgh Island, off the south coast of Devon, is only an island for a few hours around high tide, when it is separated from the beach at Bigbury-on-Sea by about 250 metres of sea. At other times, the "island" is linked to the mainland by a narrow strip of exposed sand which can easily be traversed on foot. At high tide, however, the only way visitors can reach the island (without getting wet) is by a strange conveyance known as a sea tractor.

Burgh Island

The sea tractor

Weird Tales

The island itself is scenically rocky, its one major building being a luxury hotel that became a fashionable destination in the inter-war years of the 20th century. The hotel is still there today, and retains the Art Deco atmosphere of the 1930s. During its heyday the hotel saw a number of famous visitors, including Noel Coward and Agatha Christie. The latter used Burgh Island – which she renamed Smuggler's Island – as the setting for one of her best known mystery novels, *Evil Under the Sun*, published in 1941 and featuring her famous detective Hercule Poirot.

Burgh Island Hotel

Evil Under the Sun has been adapted into other media a number of times, although not all these adaptations have been true to the Burgh Island location. Two that do remain faithful are the TV adaptation of 2001 and the Adventure Company video game of 2007 – both of which clearly depict Burgh Island and its sea tractor.

10.9 The Ring of Silvianus

Satnav: The Vyne, Hampshire RG24 9HL (National Trust)

The Vyne is a 16th century country house just outside the village of Sherborne St John, a couple of miles north Basingstoke in Hampshire. The Vyne was originally built for Lord Sandys, King Henry VIII's Lord Chamberlain. In 1653 it became the property of the Chute family, who handed it over to The National Trust in 1958. On display in the house are a number of interesting artefacts, including the "Ring of Silvianus".

The Vyne

The Ring of Silvianus, named after the Romano-British citizen who was believed to have owned it, is an inscribed gold ring dating from the 4th century. It was unearthed in 1785 in a field near the village of Silchester, about 5 miles north of Sherborne St John. Silchester is the site of the ancient Roman town of *Calleva Atrebatum*, which was first occupied by the Romans in 45 AD. Extensive sections of the town walls and an amphitheatre can still be found there today. Shortly after the ring's discovery it came into the possession of the Chute family and was held in their private collection.

The discovery of a lead tablet early in the 19th century at another Roman site, the temple of Nodens in Gloucestershire, provided some context to the ring. The tablet bears a Latin inscription which translates as follows:

> *For the God Nodens: Silvianus has lost a ring and has donated one half its worth to Nodens. Among those named Senicianus permit no good health until it is returned to the temple of Nodens.*

This appears to be a curse, accusing a person named Senicianus of stealing the ring from Silvianus!

The connection between the ring and the curse was made in 1929, by the archaeologist Sir Mortimer Wheeler. It seems that Wheeler consulted with J. R. R. Tolkien, who was a Professor of Anglo-Saxon history at Oxford University, to assist in understanding the origins of the name Nodens referred to in the curse.

Some people believe that Tolkien's experience with the Ring of Silvianus and the cursed tablet inspired his writing of *The Hobbit* and *The Lord of the Rings*.

The Ring of Silvianus

10.10 The Dalek Caves

**Satnav: Winspit Quarry, Worth Matravers, Dorset BH19 3LQ
(park in village and follow footpath to quarry)**

At one time there were numerous quarries on the Purbeck section of the Dorset coastline, which provided highly prized stone for prestigious building projects in London and elsewhere. The remains of one such quarry can be found on the cliff side at Winspit near the village of Worth Matravers. This quarry was in use until around 1940, when the site was taken over for use as part of the south coast's naval and air defences during the Second World War. Today the quarry and surrounding cliff are open to the public to explore and climb.

Winspit Quarry

Winspit Quarry may have a familiar look to many TV viewers, because it has often been used as a filming location. For example, the quarry was used in the *Dr Who* adventure "The Underwater Menace" in 1967, which saw the second Doctor (Patrick Troughton) encounter a band of survivors from Atlantis on a supposedly deserted volcanic island.

More famously, the fourth Doctor (Tom Baker) also visited Winspit in 1979 for "The Destiny of the Daleks". In this instance the quarry portrayed the planet D-5-Gamma-Z-Alpha – better known as Skaro, the home world of the Daleks! The quarry's ruined buildings provided a suitably bleak representation of what an abandoned Dalek city might look like.

The ruined buildings

Inside Winspit's "caves"

Index

Arch – Chapter 1: *Weird Archaeology*	Leg – Chapter 6: *Weird Legends*
Buil – Chapter 2: *Weird Buildings*	Rel – Chapter 7: *Weird Religion*
Con – Chapter 3: *Weird Constructions*	Sci – Chapter 8: *Weird Science*
Hist – Chapter 4: *Weird History*	Sec – Chapter 9: *Weird Secrets*
Land – Chapter 5: *Weird Landscape*	Tale – Chapter 10: *Weird Tales*

Abbotts Ann (Hants) - Rel 10
Abbotsbury (Dorset) - Sci 7
Alton (Hants) - Hist 6
Alton Barnes (Wilts) - Land 6
Athelney (Somerset) - Leg 6
Avebury (Wilts) - Arch 3
Basingstoke Canal (Hants) - Sec 6
Bath (Somerset) - Arch 7
Beer Quarry (Devon) - Sec 4
Bishops Cannings (Wilts) - Rel 6
Bournemouth (Dorset) - Sci 4
Brean Down Fort (Somerset) - Sci 6
Broad Town (Wilts) - Land 9
Brockenhurst (Hants) - Leg 10
Burgh Island (Devon) - Tale 8
Cadbury Castle (Somerset) - Leg 4
Castle Drogo (Devon) - Buil 7
Cerne Giant (Dorset) - Land 7
Chard (Somerset) - Sci 5
Charmouth (Dorset) - Sci 1
Cheddar Gorge (Somerset) - Arch 1
Chesapeake Mill (Hants) - Buil 9
Clouds Hill (Dorset) - Tale 6
Combe Gibbet (Berks) - Con 2
Crewkerne (Somerset) - Rel 7
Danebury (Hants) - Land 2
Dartmoor (Devon) - Tale 4

Dorchester (Dorset) - Arch 8
Dunster Castle (Somerset) - Sec 5
East Coker (Somerset) - Tale 2
Exeter (Devon) - Buil 10
Fanny Adams (Hants) - Leg 9
Farley Down (Hants) - Con 5
Glastonbury Abbey (Somerset) - Arch 9
Glastonbury Tor (Somerset) - Leg 3
Great Wishford (Wilts) - Hist 9
Grovely Wood (Wilts) - Sec 8
Ham Hill (Somerset) - Land 4
Harewood Forest (Hants) - Hist 1
Hell Stone (Dorset) - Arch 6
Highclere Castle (Berks) - Tale 7
Honeystreet (Wilts) - Sci 10
Horton Tower (Dorset) - Con 4
Imber (Wilts) - Sec 1
Kilve (Somerset) - Con 8
Kimmeridge (Dorset) - Con 9
Kingston Lacy (Dorset) - Arch 10
Knowlton (Dorset) - Rel 1
Langport (Somerset) - Buil 6
Langton Cross (Dorset) - Rel 4
Ludgershall Castle (Wilts) - Hist 3
Lyme Regis Museum (Dorset) - Buil 8

Maiden Castle (Dorset) - Land 3
Malmesbury Abbey (Wilts) - Sci 2
Maud Heath Causeway (Wilts) - Con 1
Monmouth Beach (Dorset) - Hist 7
Montacute (Somerset) - Tale 5
Morwhellham Quay (Devon) - Hist 10
Muchelney (Somerset) - Rel 5
Nether Wallop (Hants) - Rel 8
New Forest (Hants) - Con 7
Old Sarum (Wilts) - Land 1
Osmington (Dorset) - Land 8
Plymouth (Devon) - Leg 2
Portesham (Dorset) - Rel 9
Portland (Dorset) - Sec 7
Portsmouth (Hants) - Con 6
Royal Signals Museum (Dorset) - Sec 9
Rufus Stone (Hants) - Hist 2
Saint Aldhelm's Chapel (Dorset) - Buil 5
Sedgemoor (Somerset) - Hist 8
Sevenhampton (Wilts) - Sec 10
Shebbear (Devon) - Leg 7
Sherborne (Dorset) - Tale 1
Solstice Park (Wilts) - Con 10
Stanton Drew (Somerset) - Arch 4
Stockwood (Dorset) - Buil 2
Stoke sub Hamdon (Somerset) - Rel 3
Stonehenge (Wilts) - Arch 2
Stourhead (Wilts) - Con 3
Sutton Bingham (Somerset) - Sec 3
Tedworth House (Wilts) - Leg 8
The Vyne (Hants) - Tale 9
Totnes (Devon) - Leg 1
Tyneham (Dorset) - Sec 2
Uffington (Berks) - Arch 5
Undercliff (Dorset) - Land 10
Verwood (Hants) - Hist 4
Warminster (Wilts) - Sci 9
Watchet (Somerset) - Tale 3
Wells Cathedral (Somerset) - Buil 1
Westbury (Wilts) - Land 5
Weymouth (Dorset) - Hist 5
Whitchurch Canonicorum (Dorset) - Rel 2
Wickham (Berks) - Buil 4
Wilsford cum Lake (Wilts) - Sci 8
Wilton (Wilts) - Buil 3
Wimborne Minster (Dorset) - Sci 3
Winchester (Hants) - Leg 5
Winspit Quarry (Dorset) - Tale 10

CFZ PUBLISHING GROUP

The World's Weirdest Publishing Group!

www.cfzpublishing.co.uk

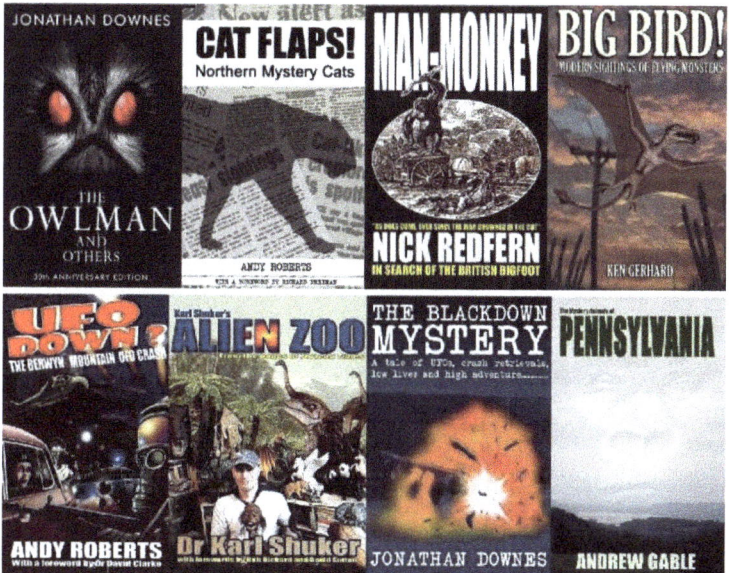

CFZ Press

Fortean Words

Fortean Fiction

CFZ Classics

Animals & Men

Journal of Cryptoozology

www.ingramcontent.com/pod-product-compliance
Lightning Source LLC
Chambersburg PA
CBHW060515090426
42735CB00011B/2236

9781909488359